Copyright © [2023] by Cindy Riesenberg

All rights reserved.

No portion of this book may be reproduced, distributed or transmitted in any form without written permission from the publisher or author, except as permitted by U.S. copyright law.

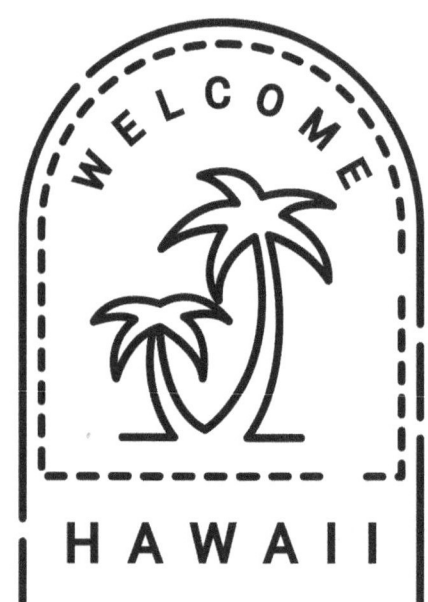

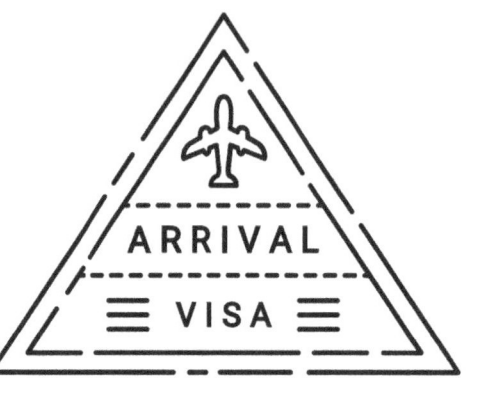

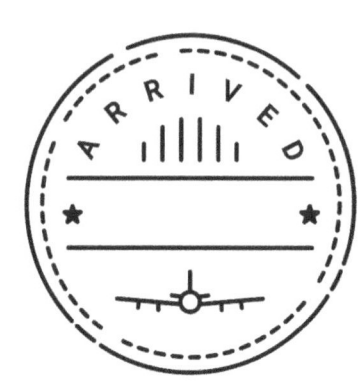

This Book Belongs To:

_____

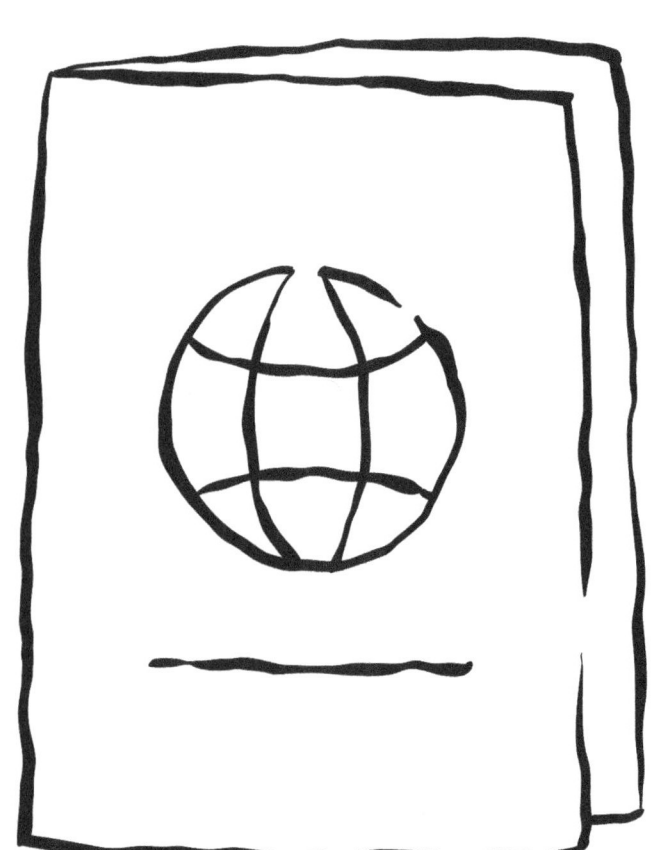

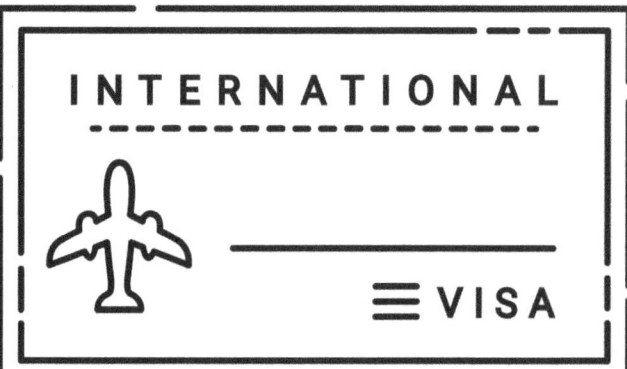

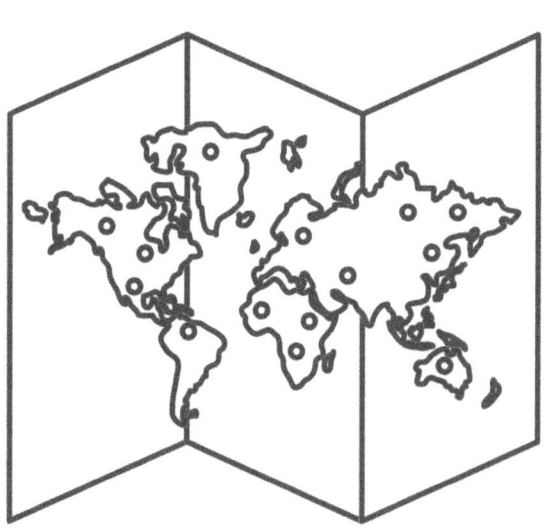

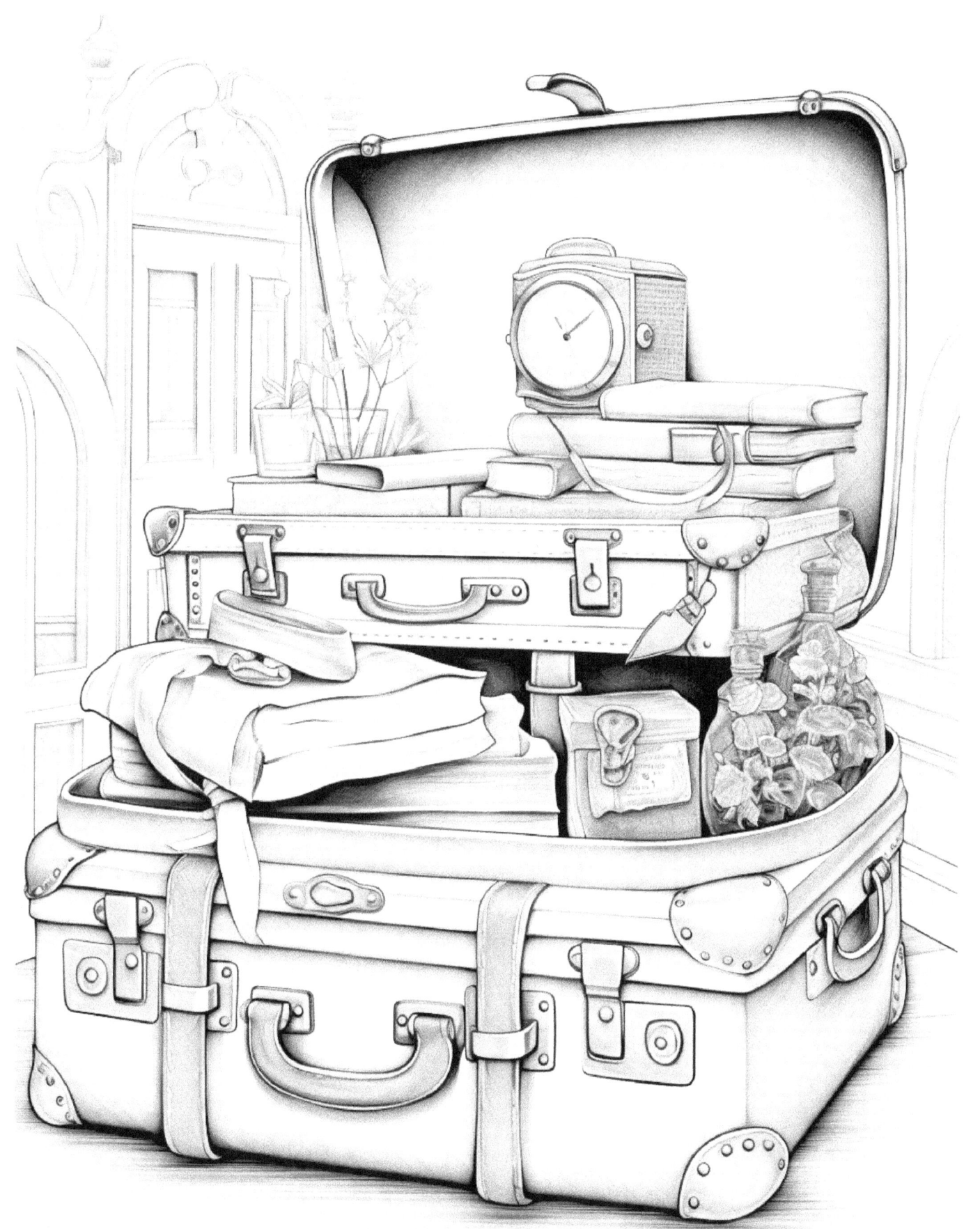

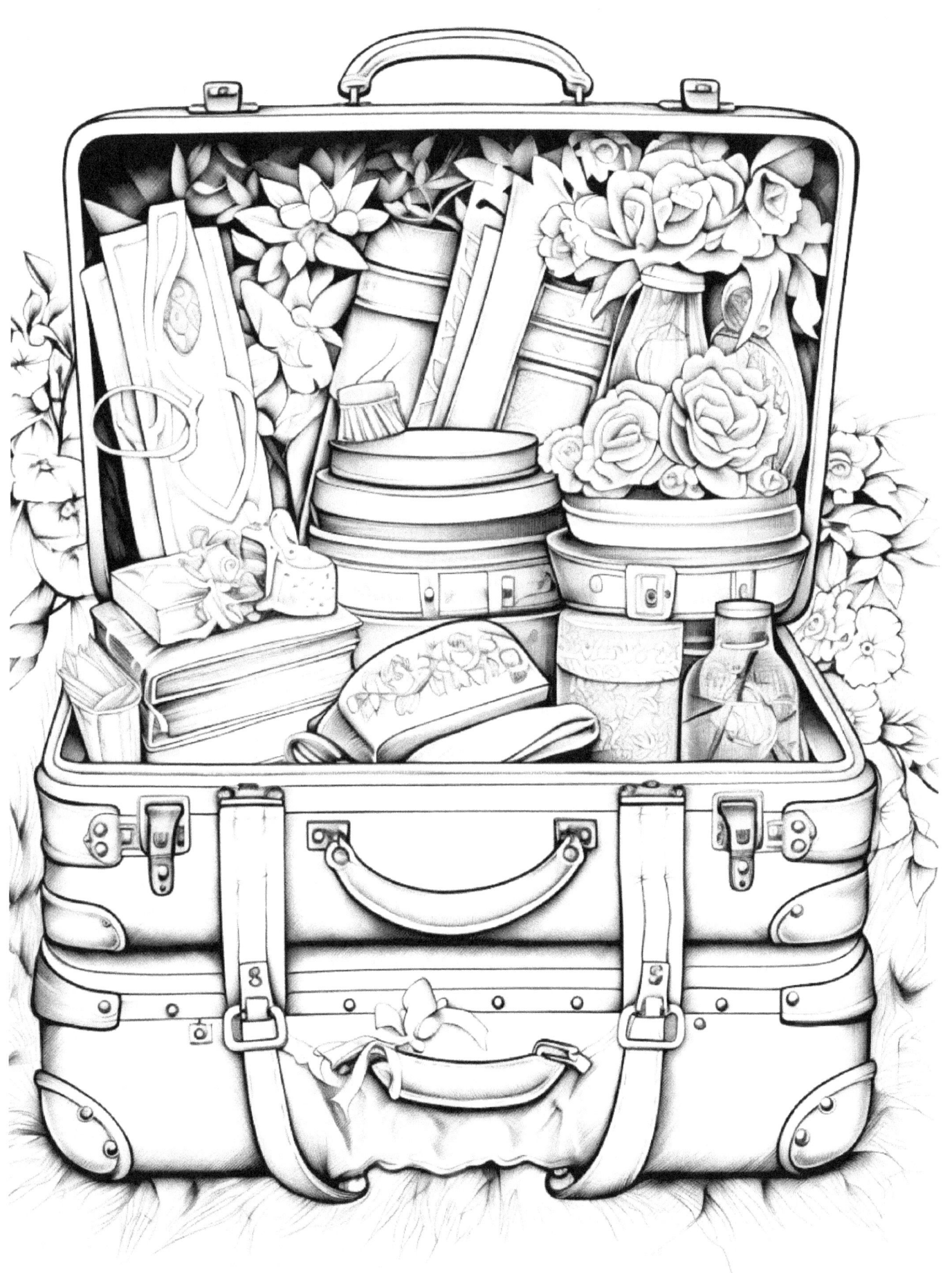

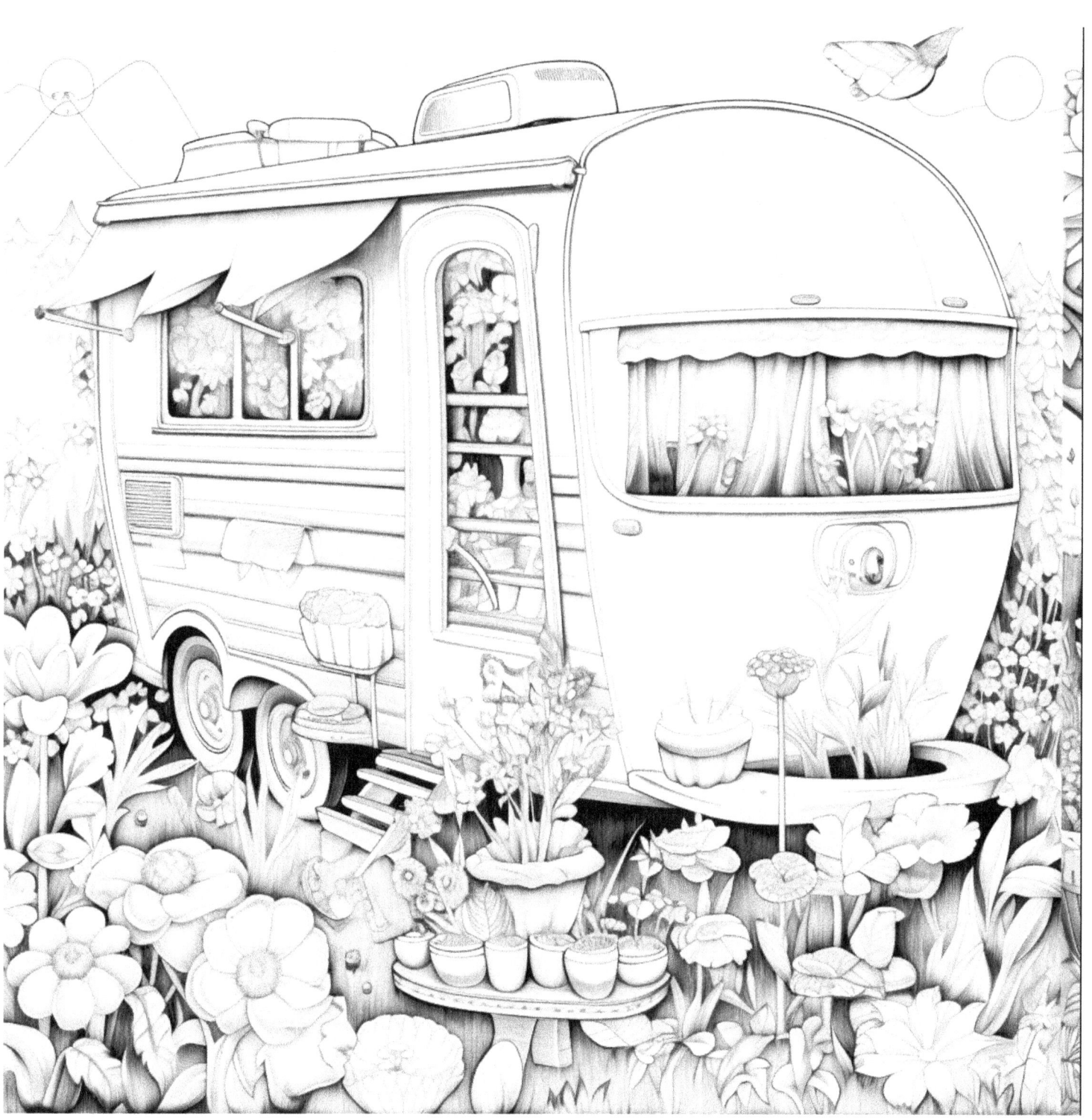

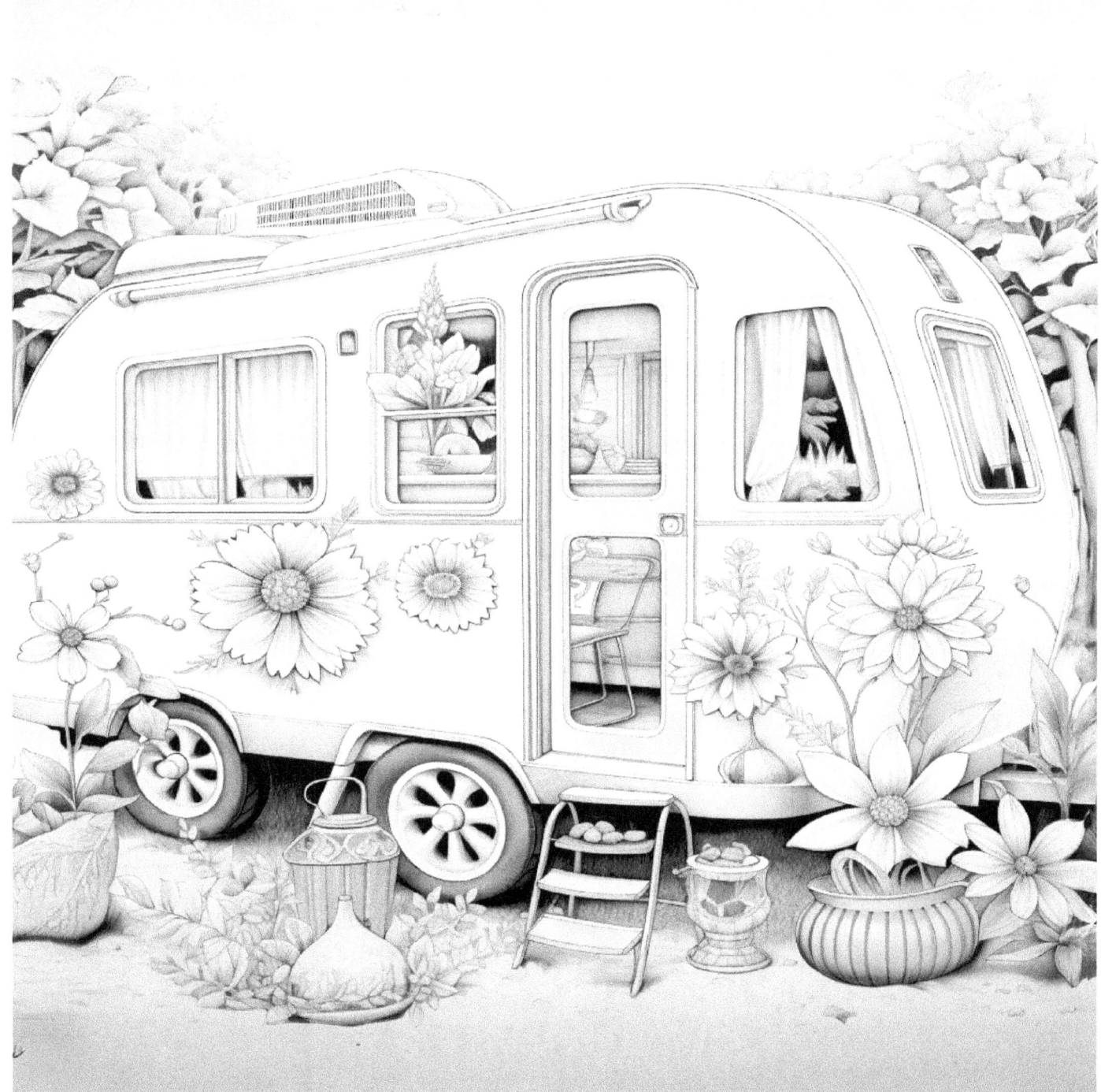

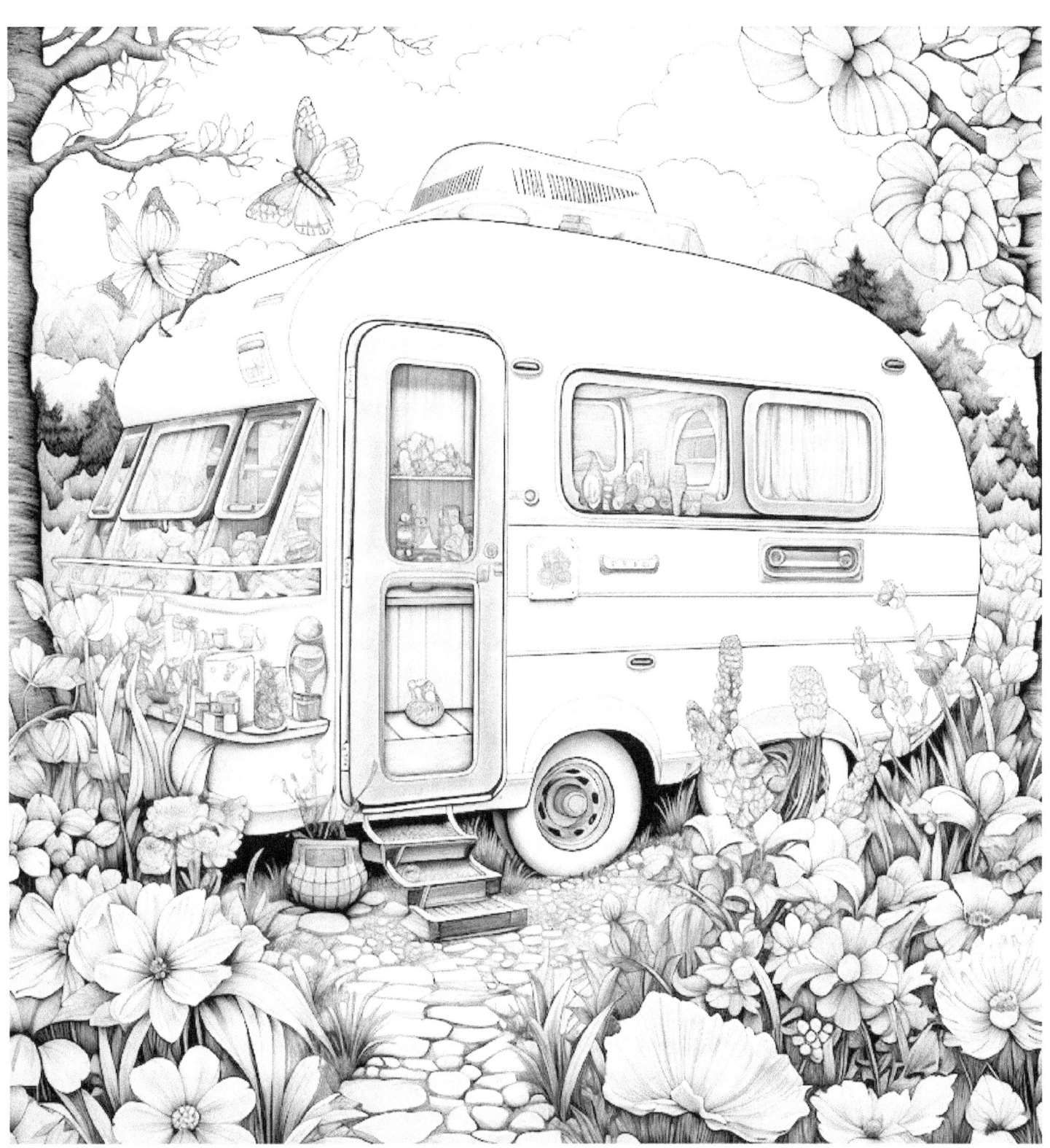

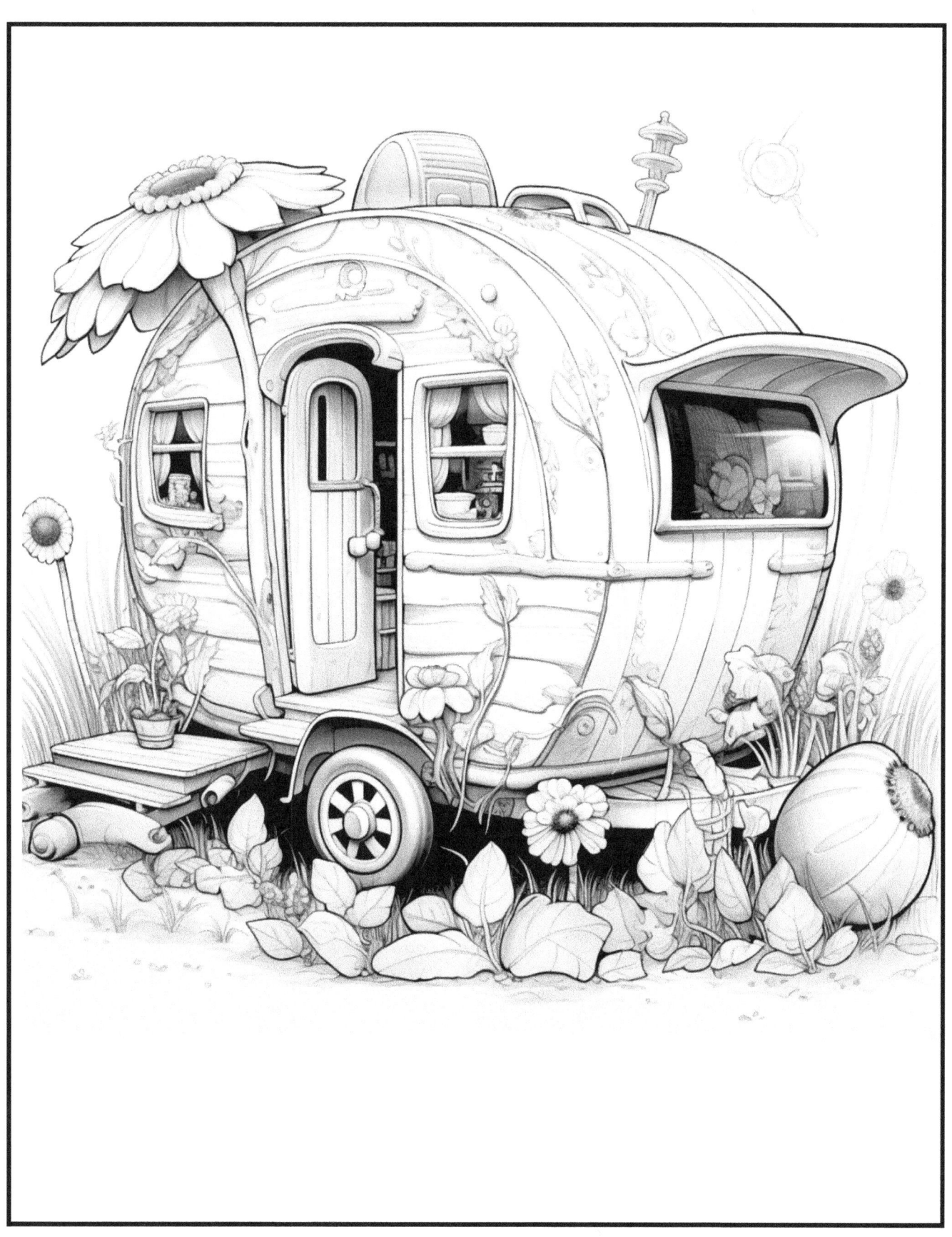

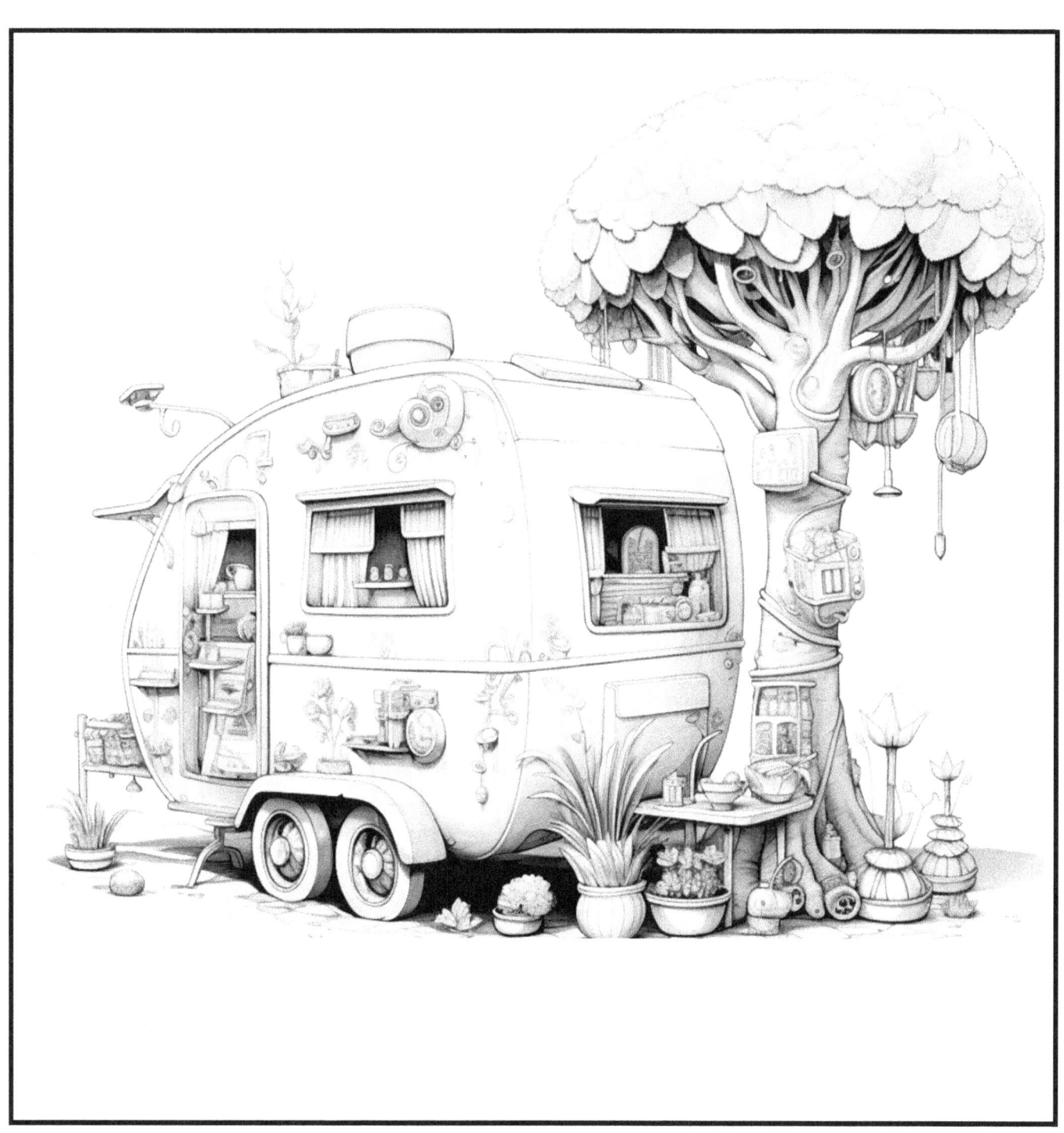

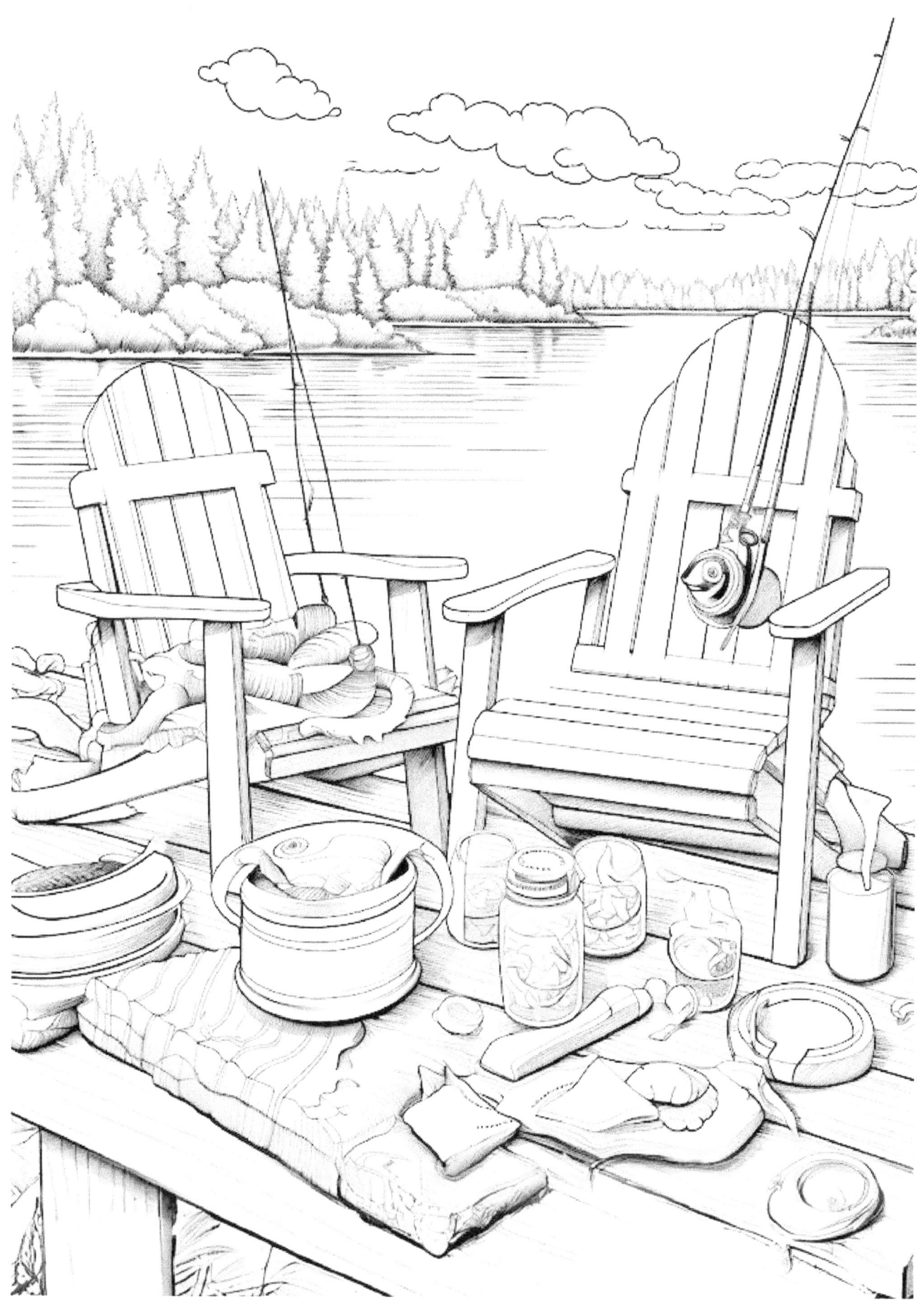

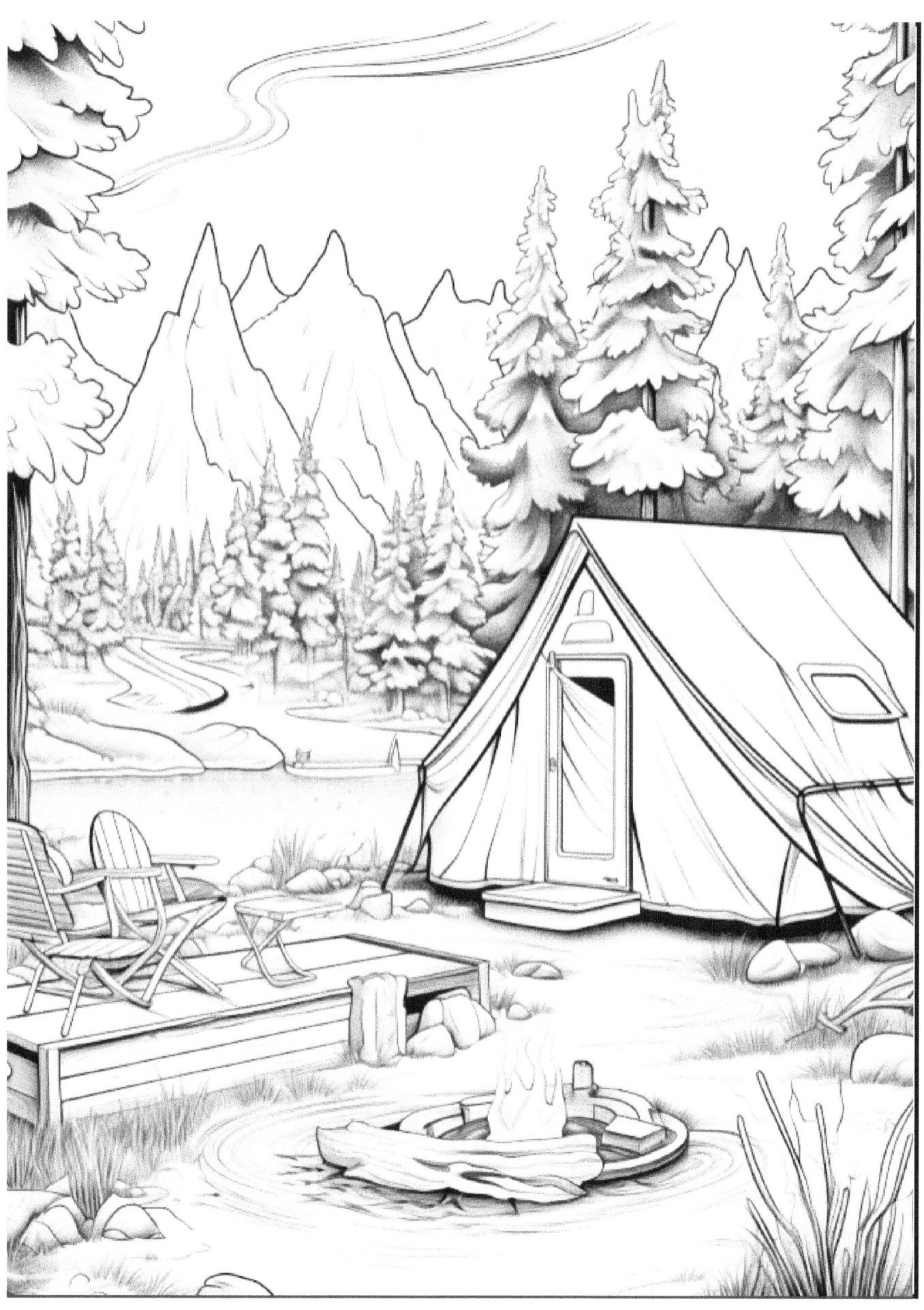

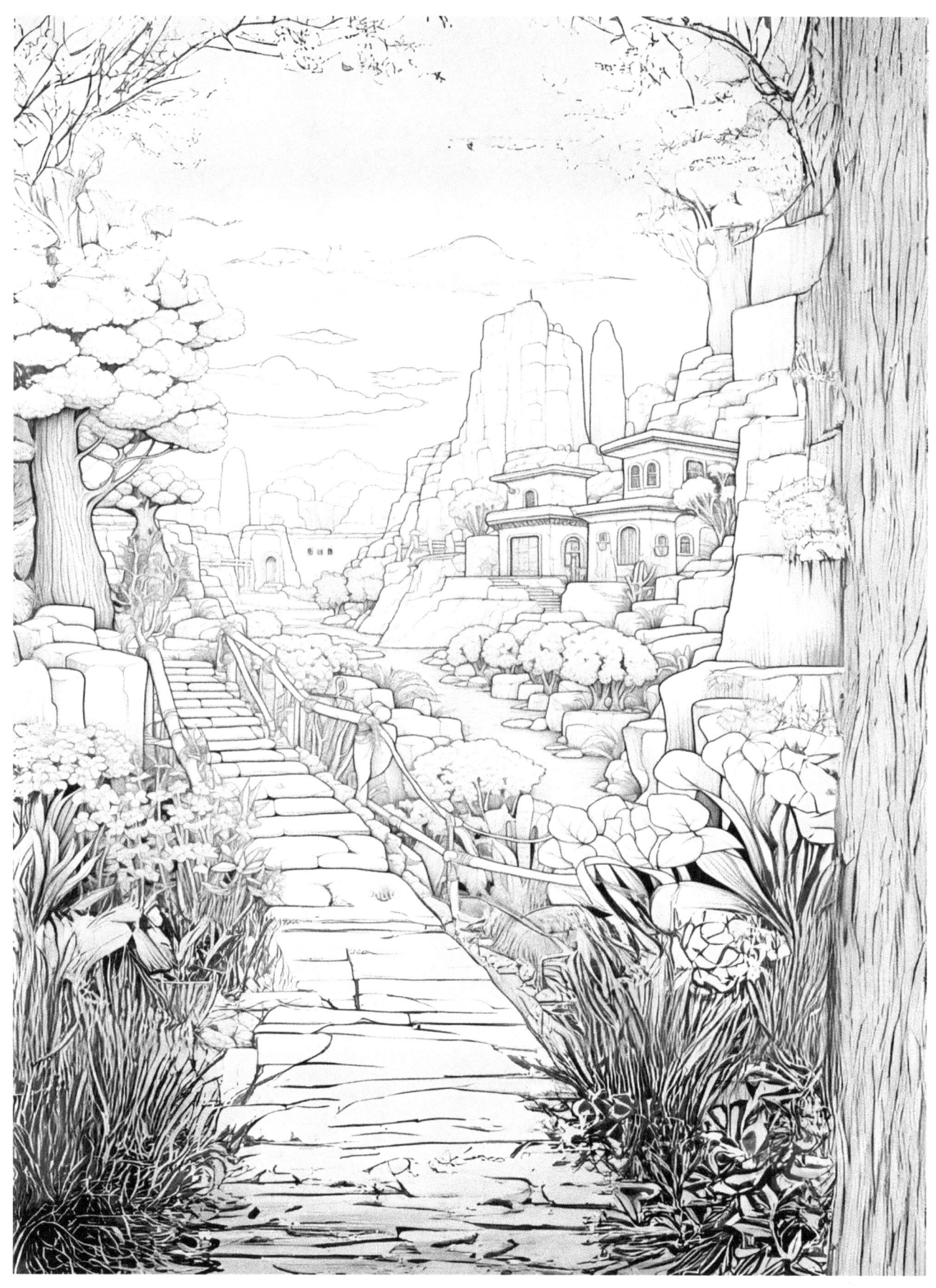

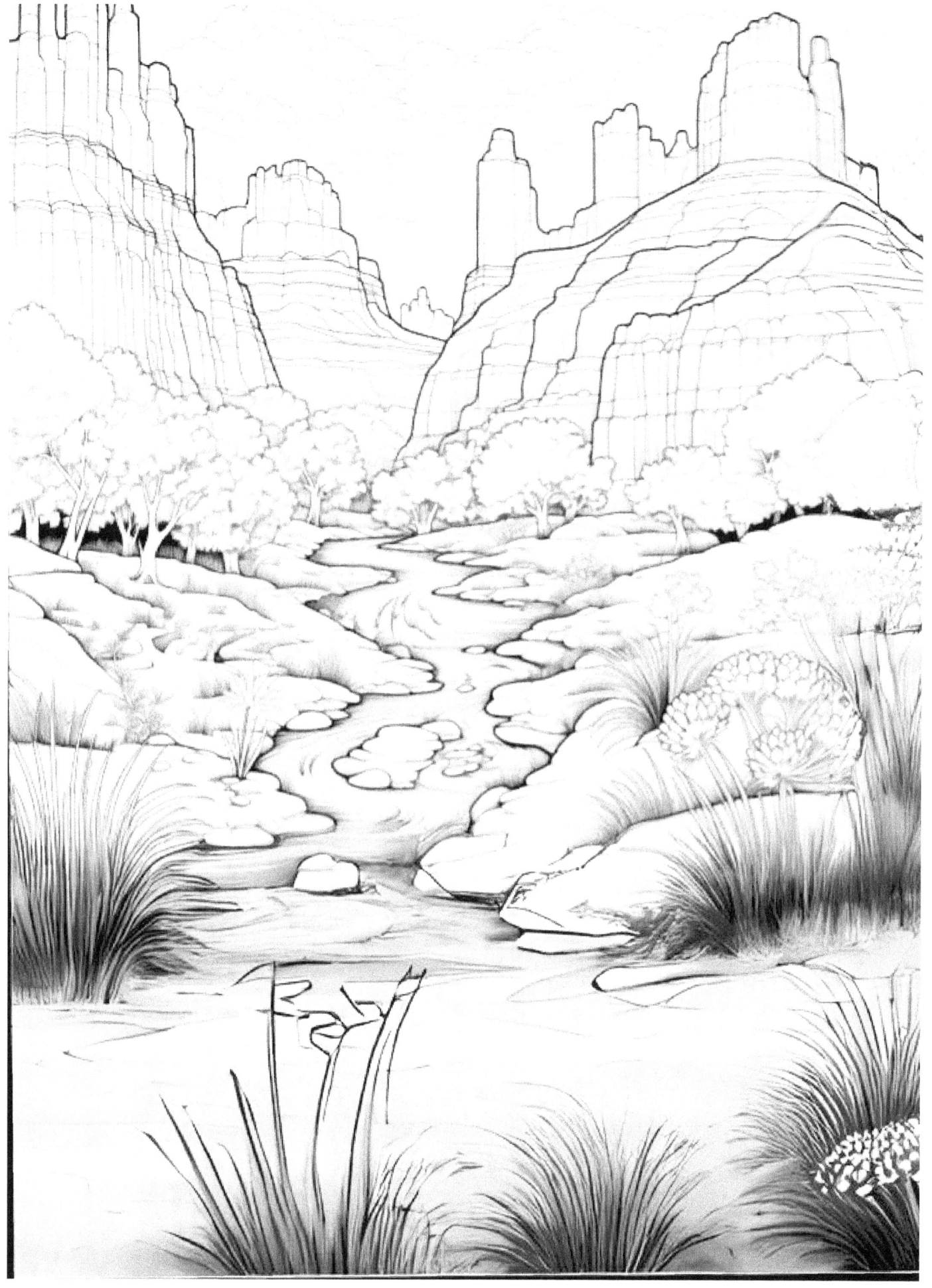

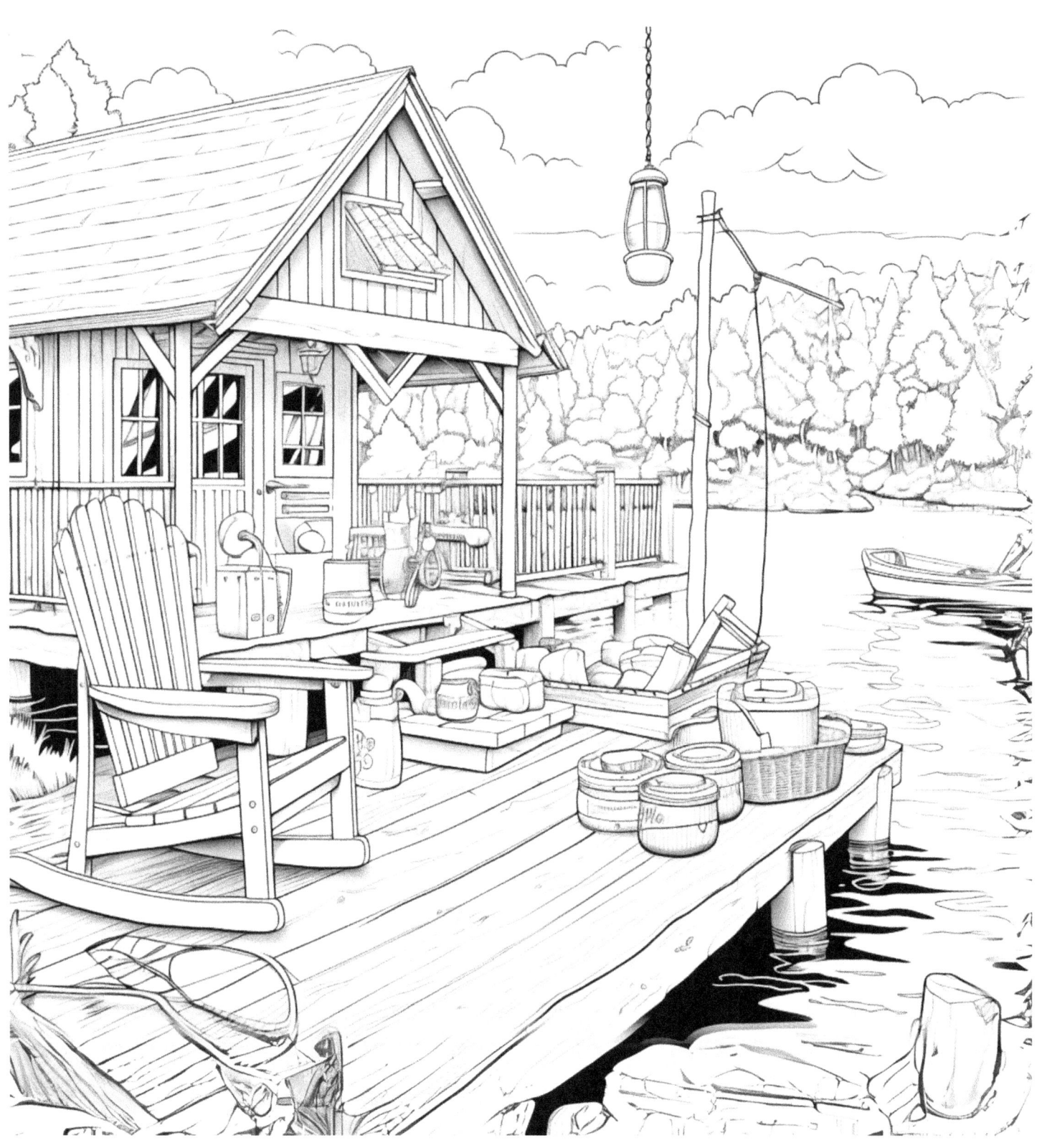

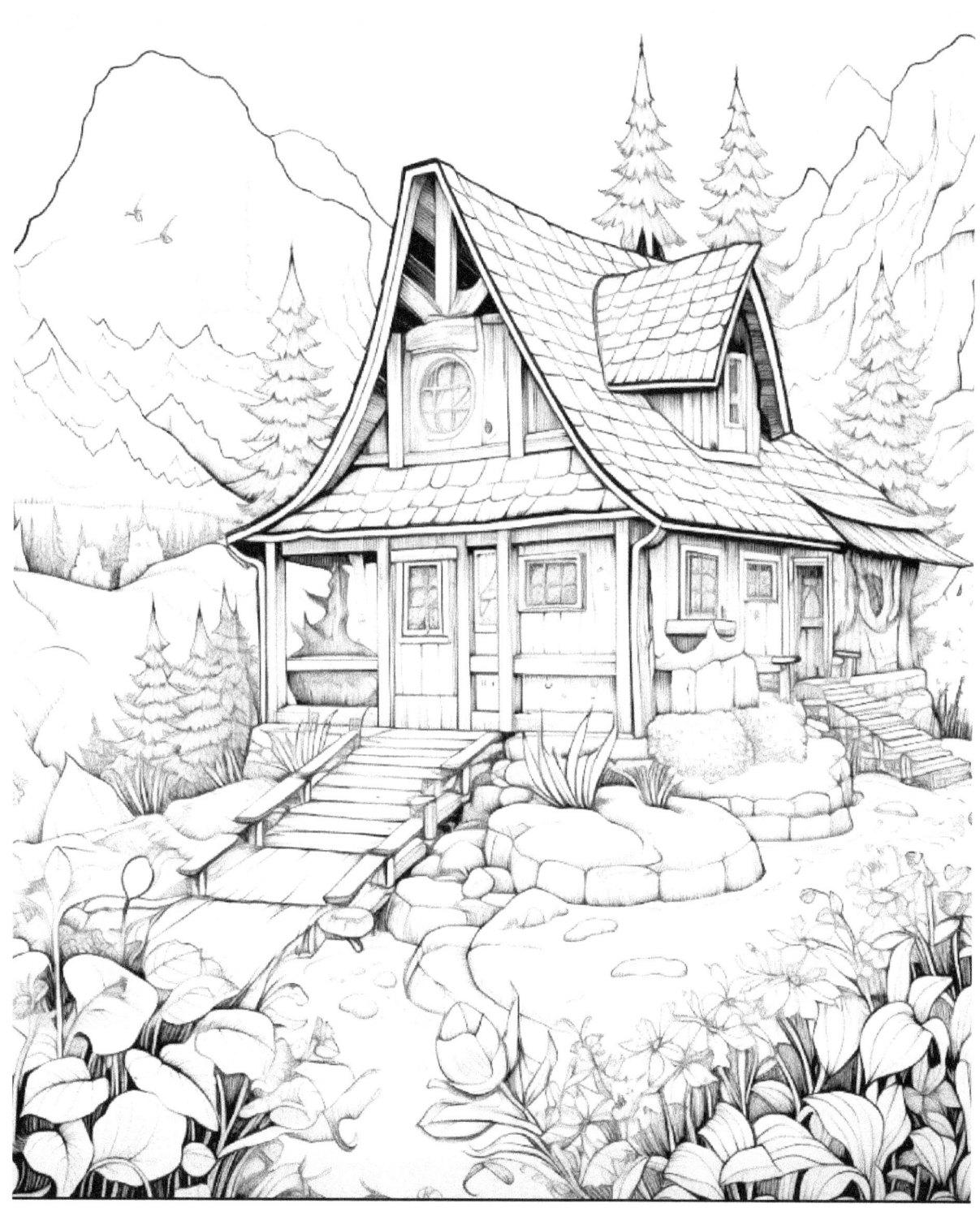

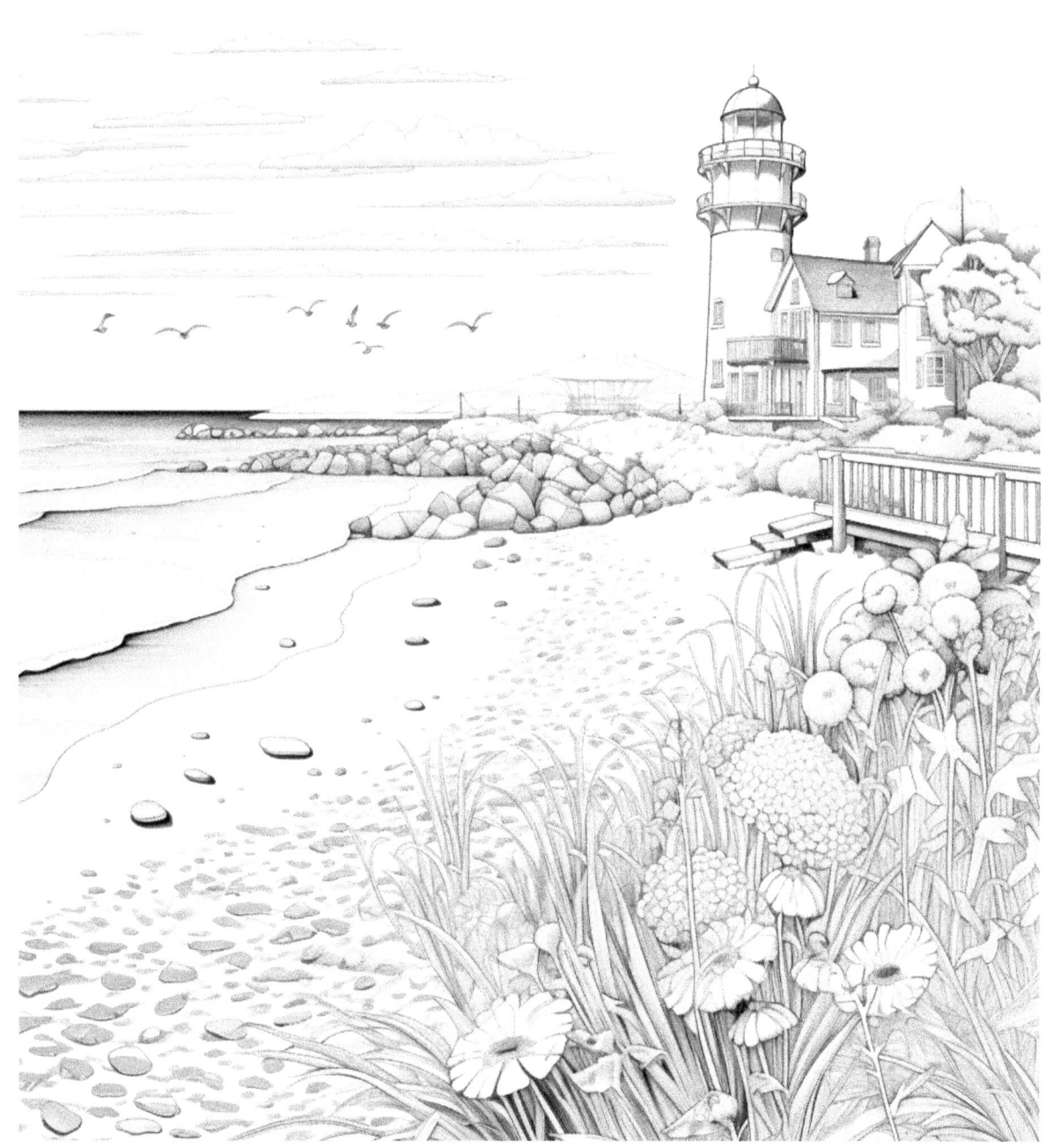

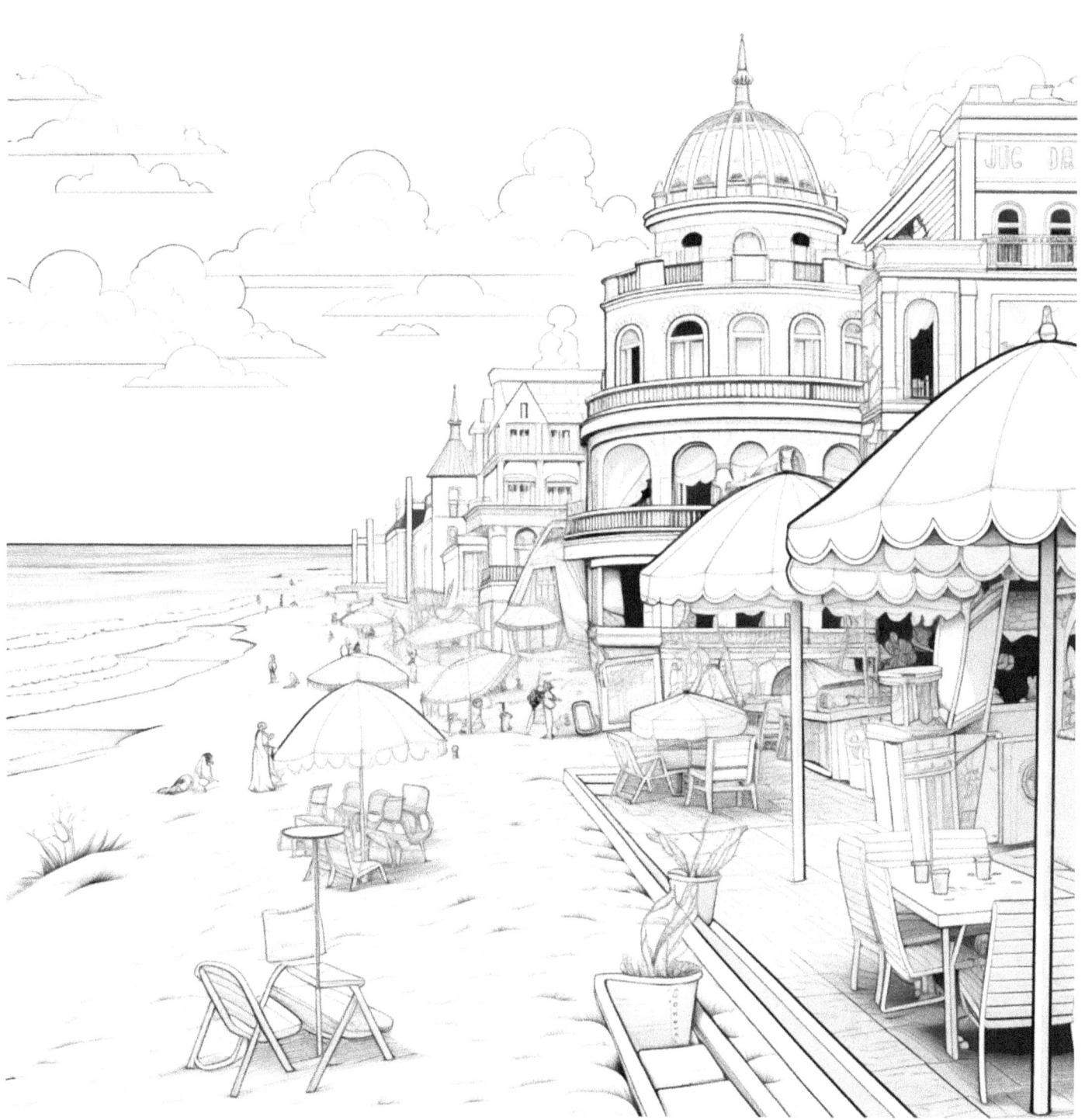

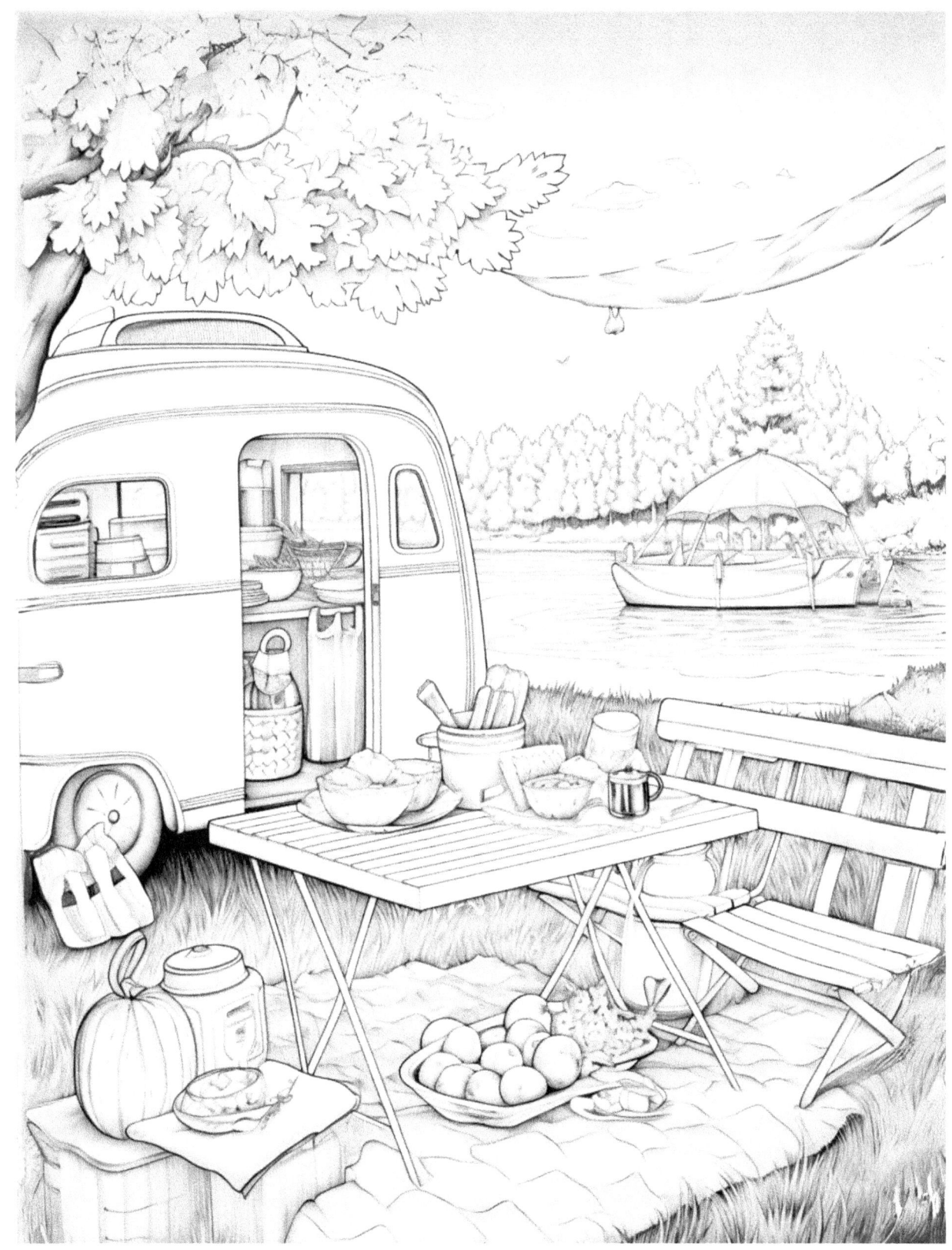

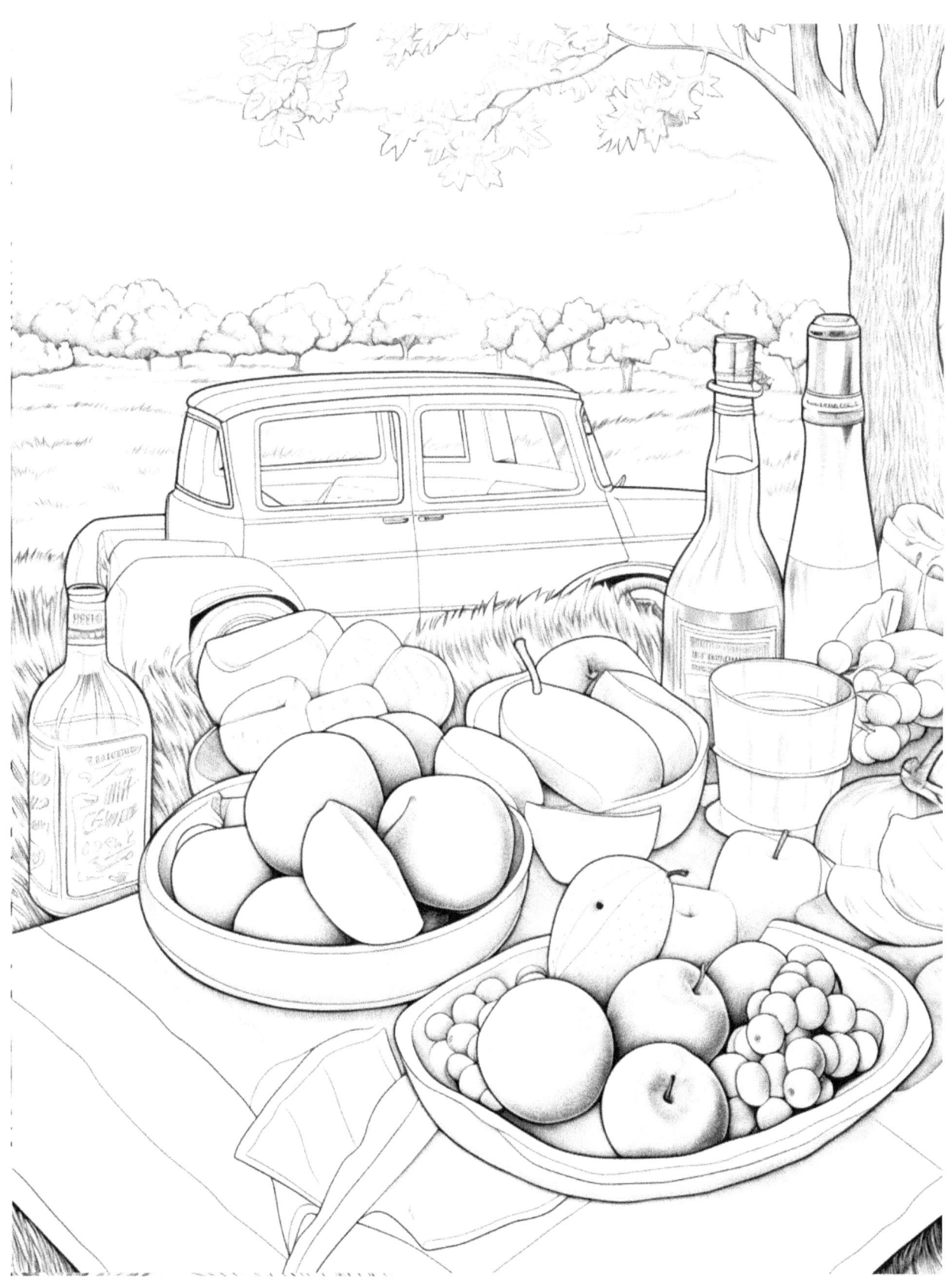

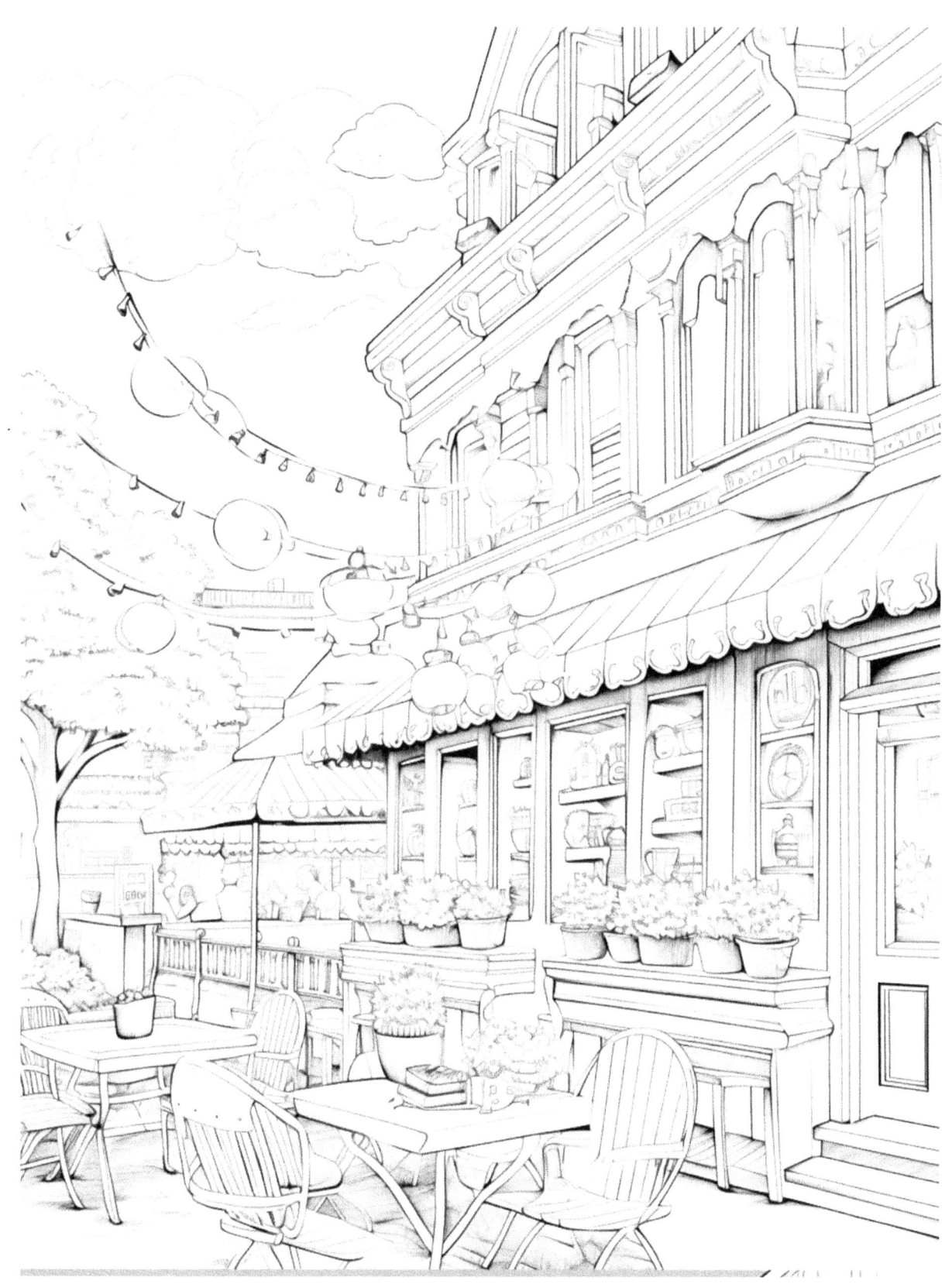

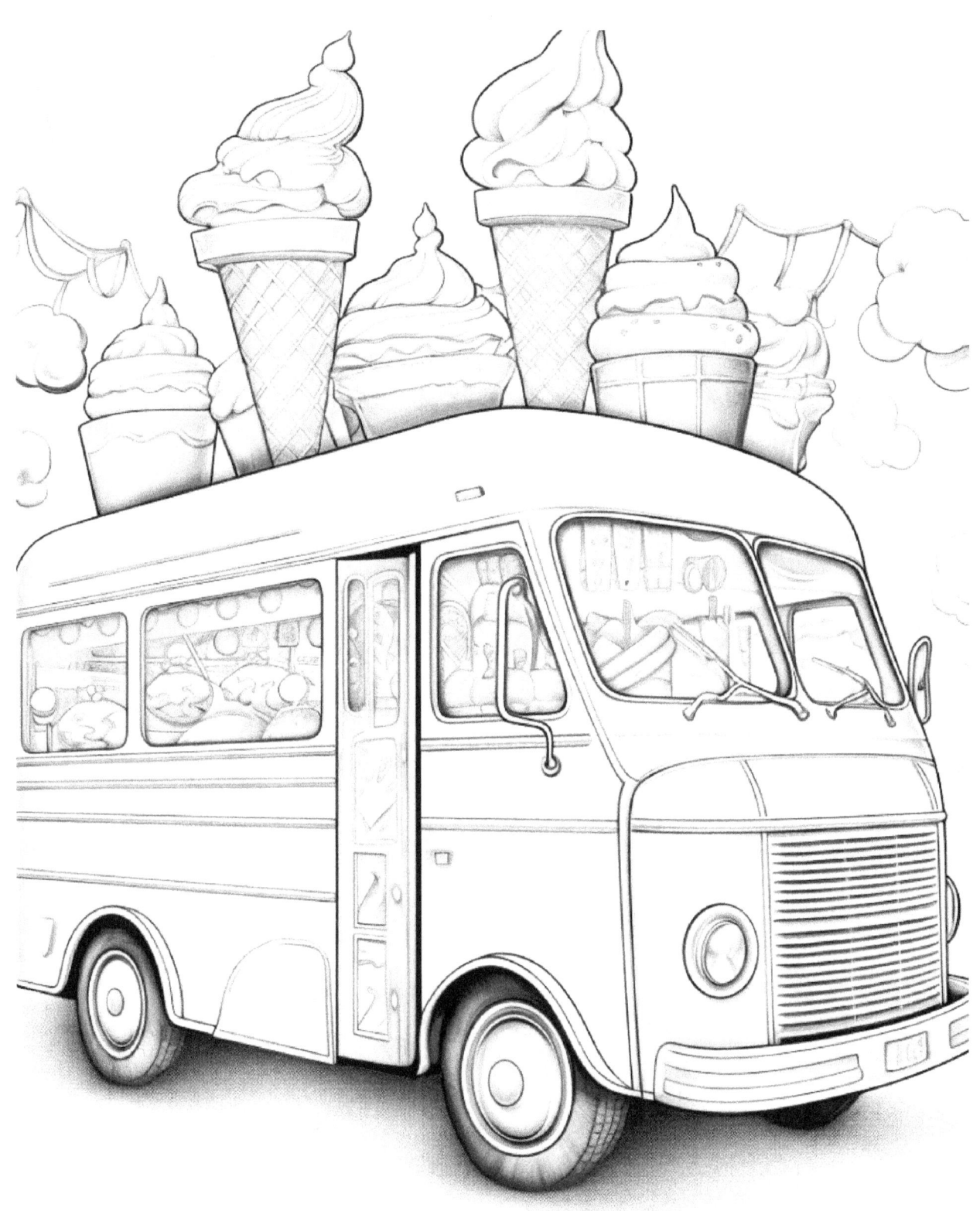

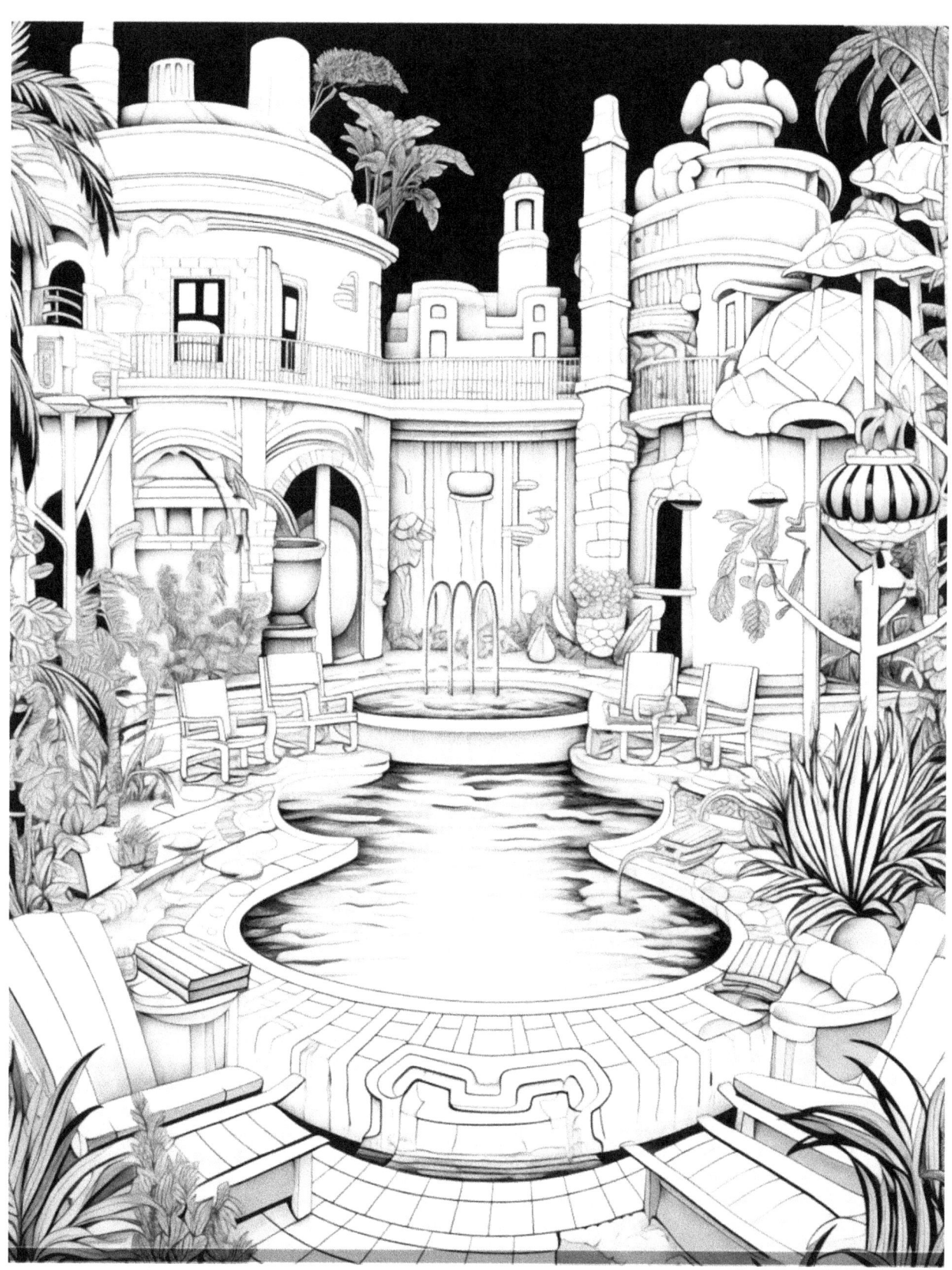

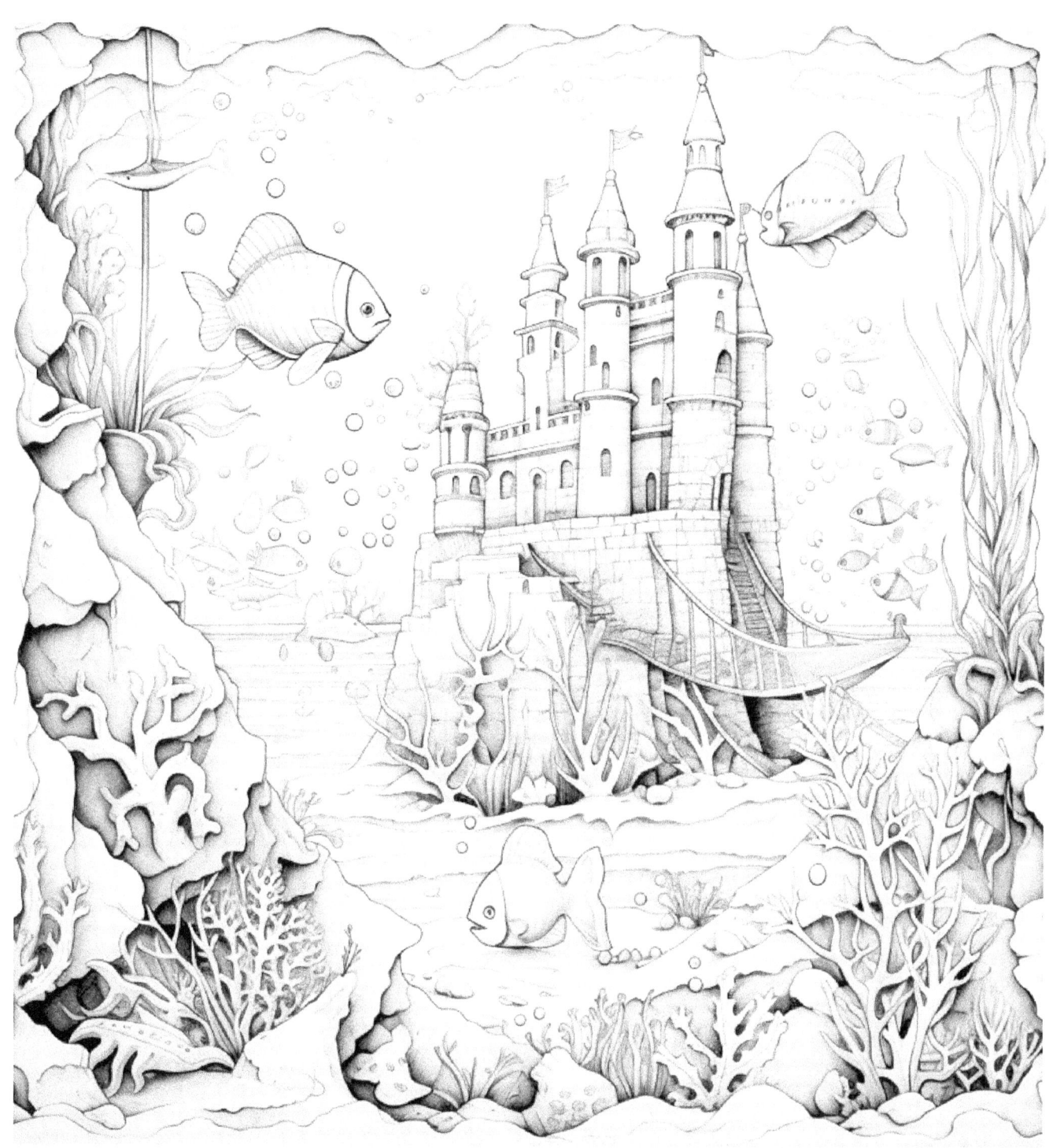

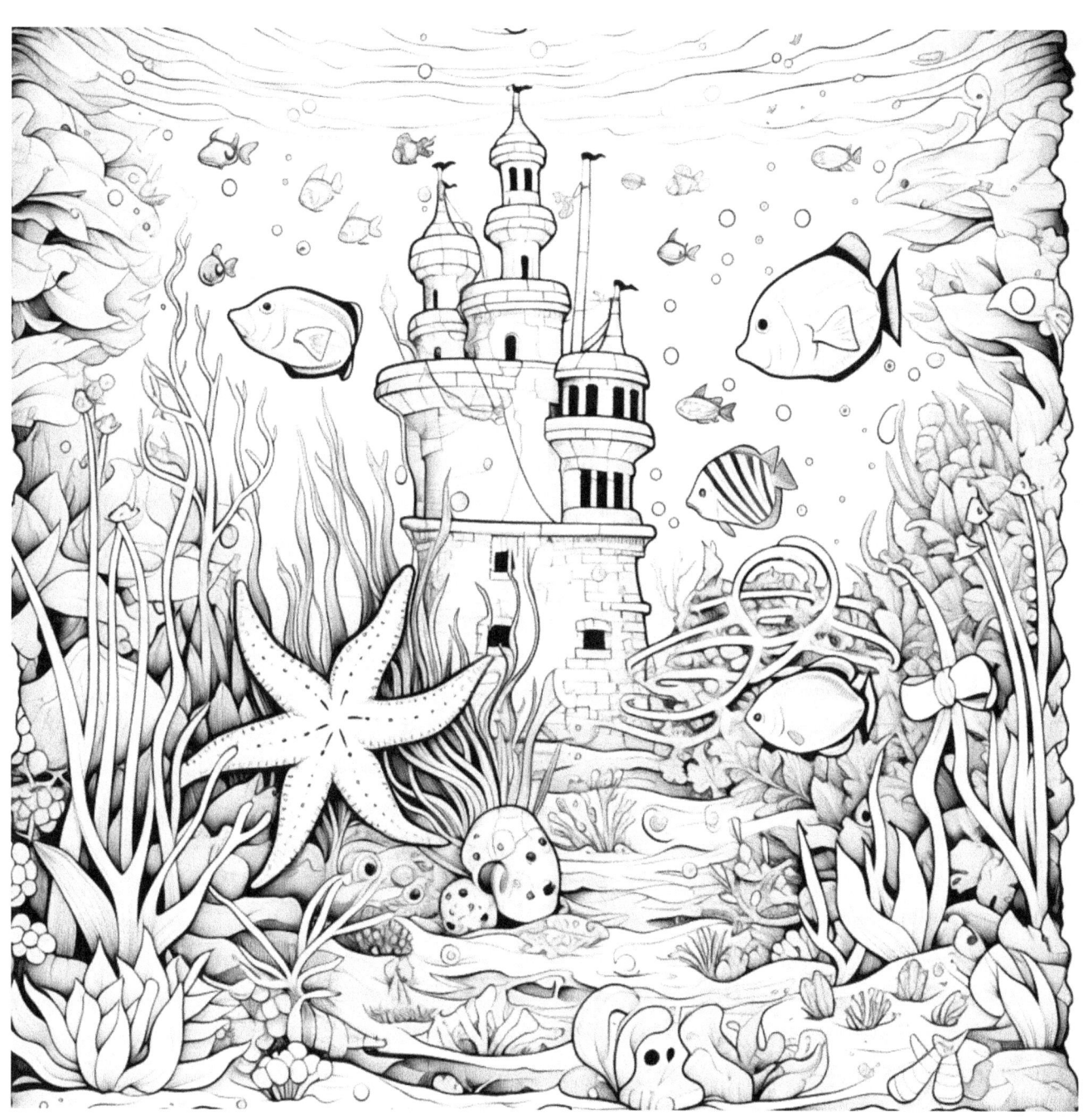

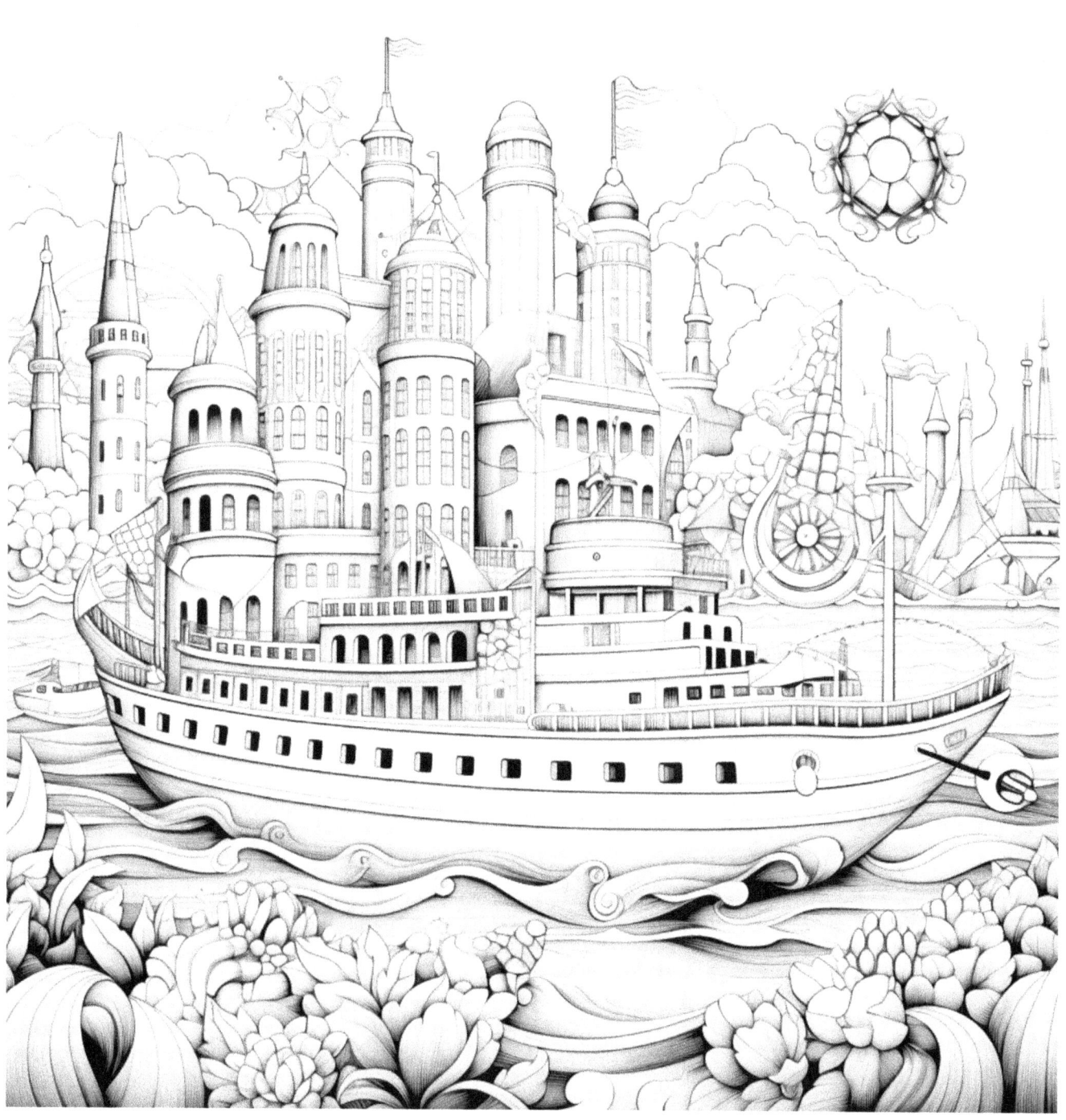

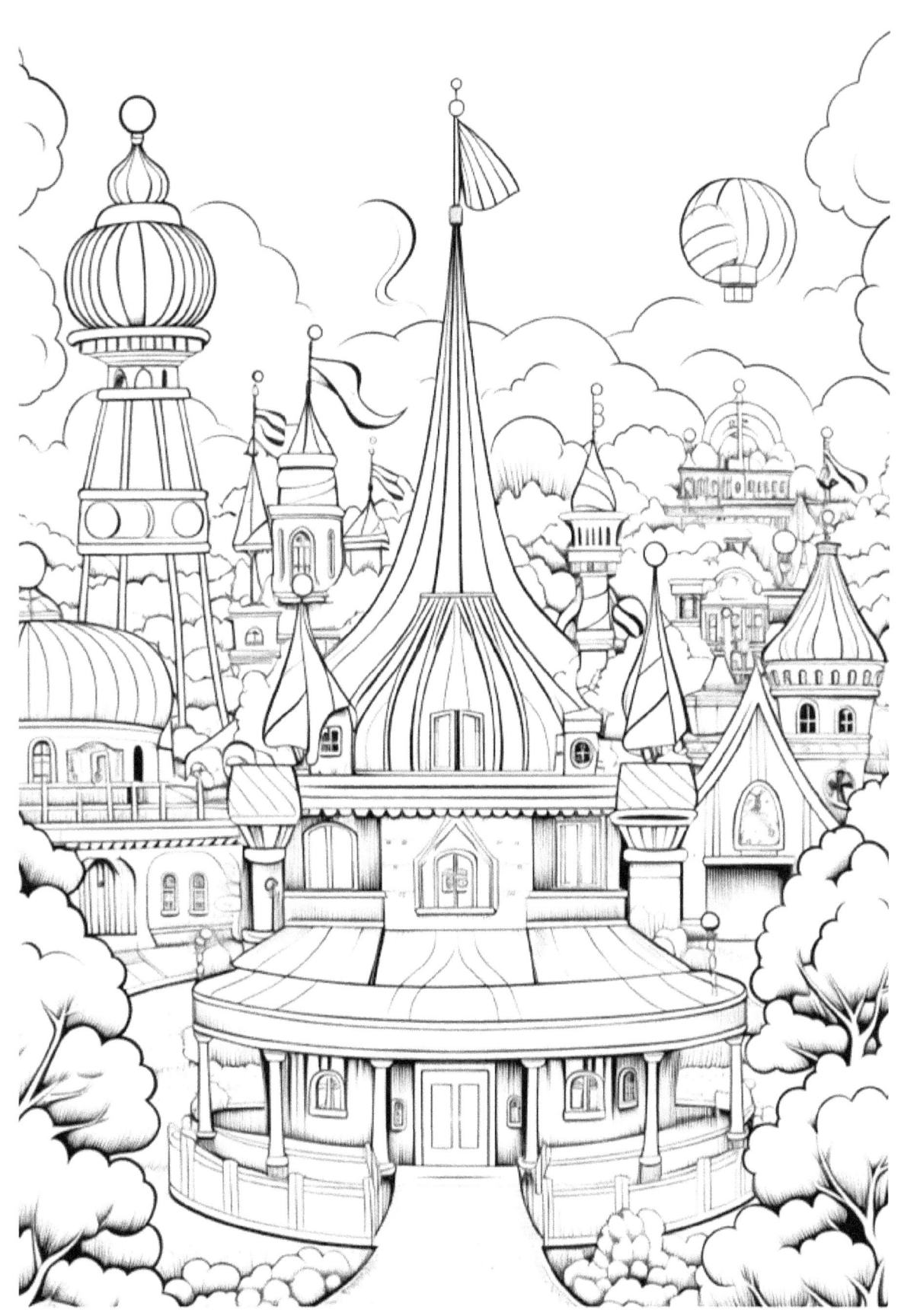

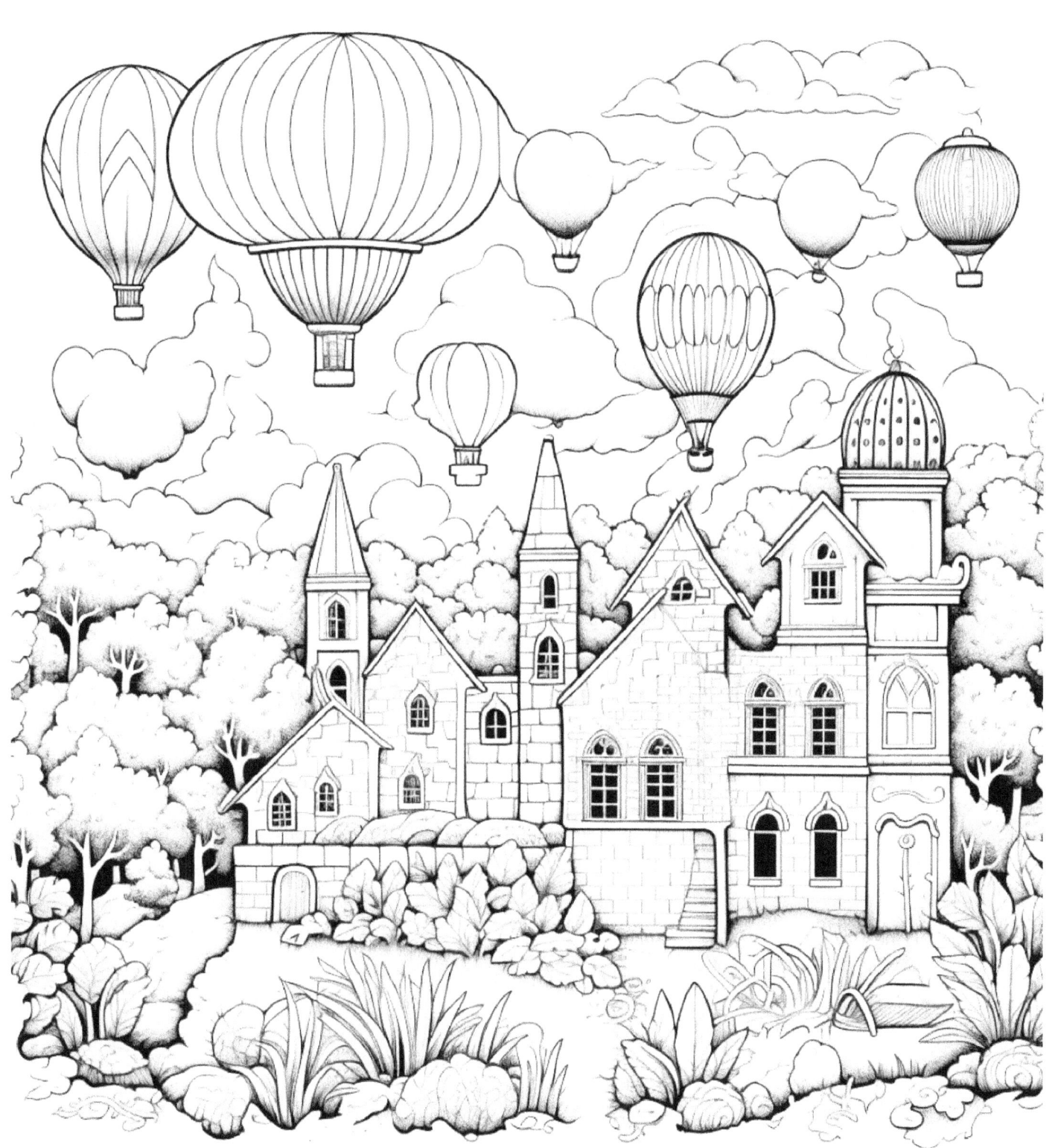

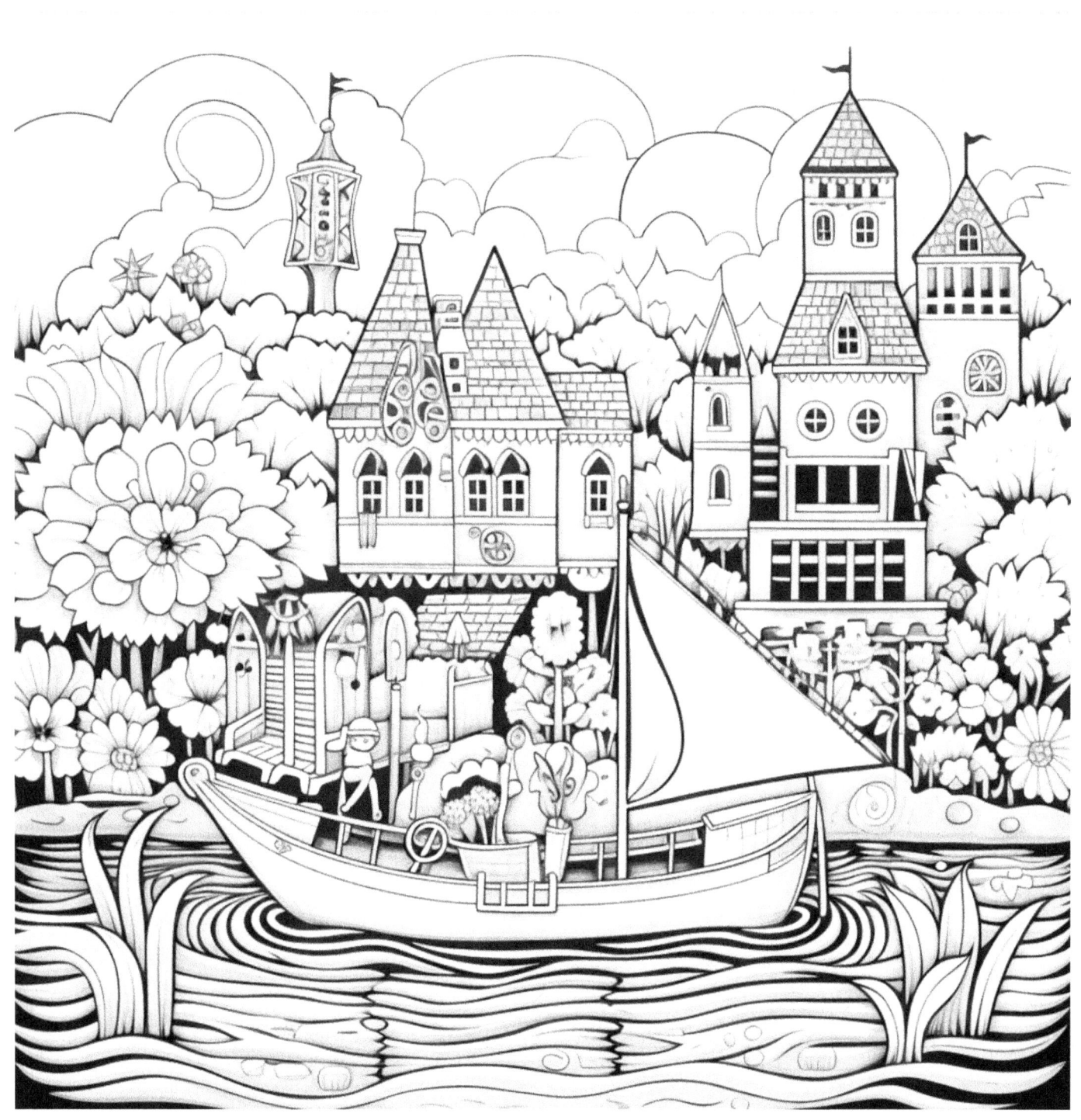

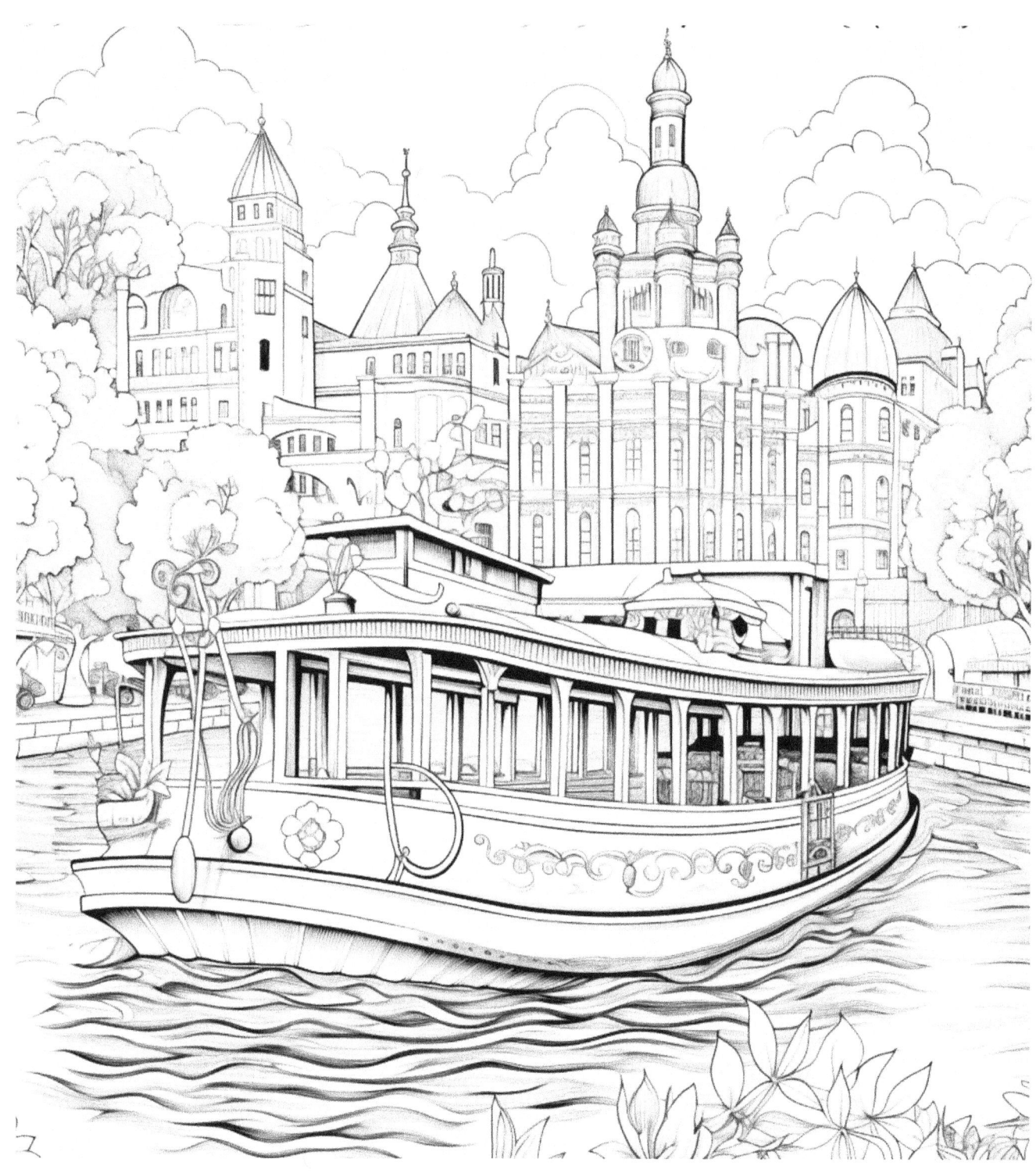

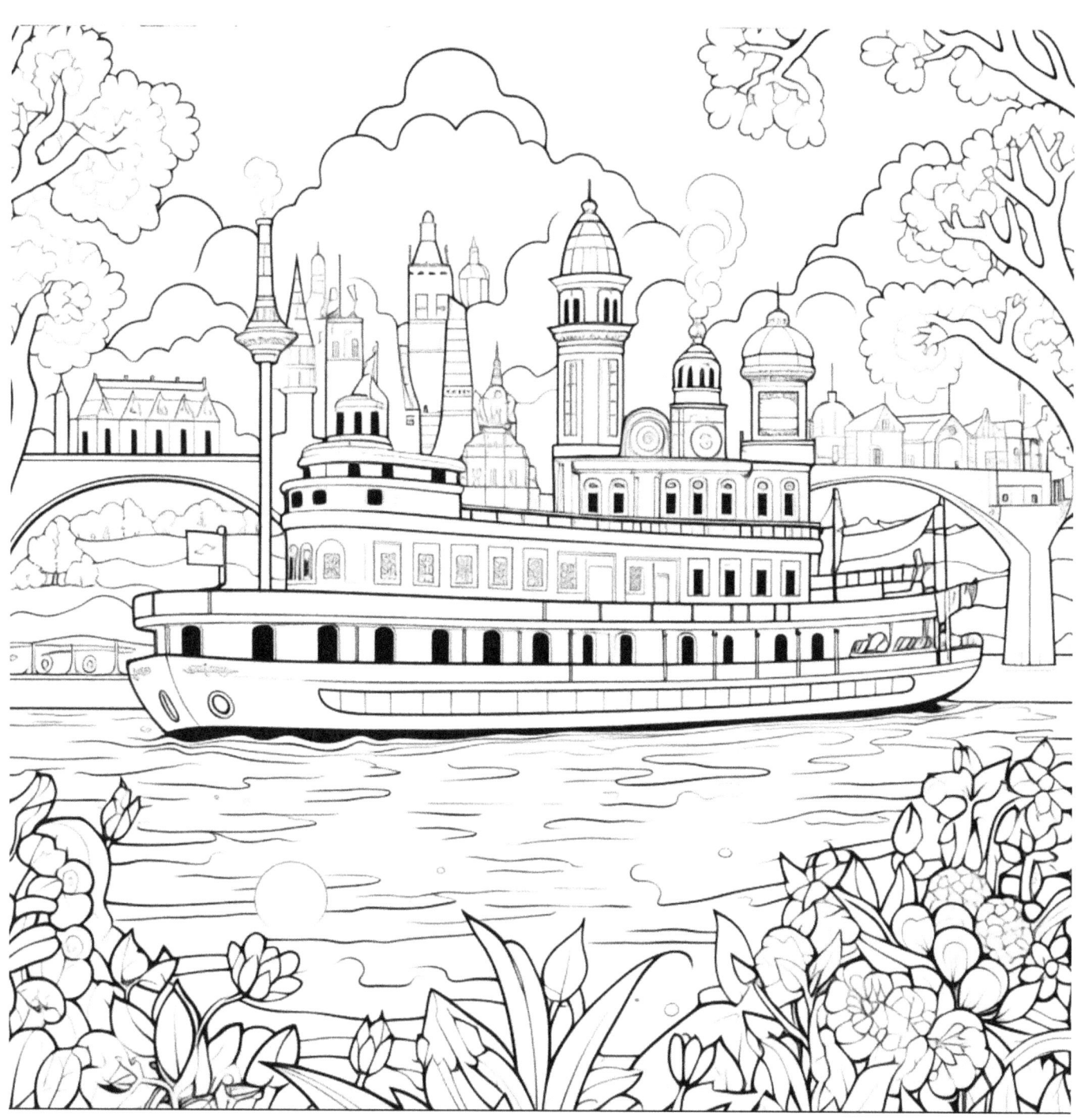

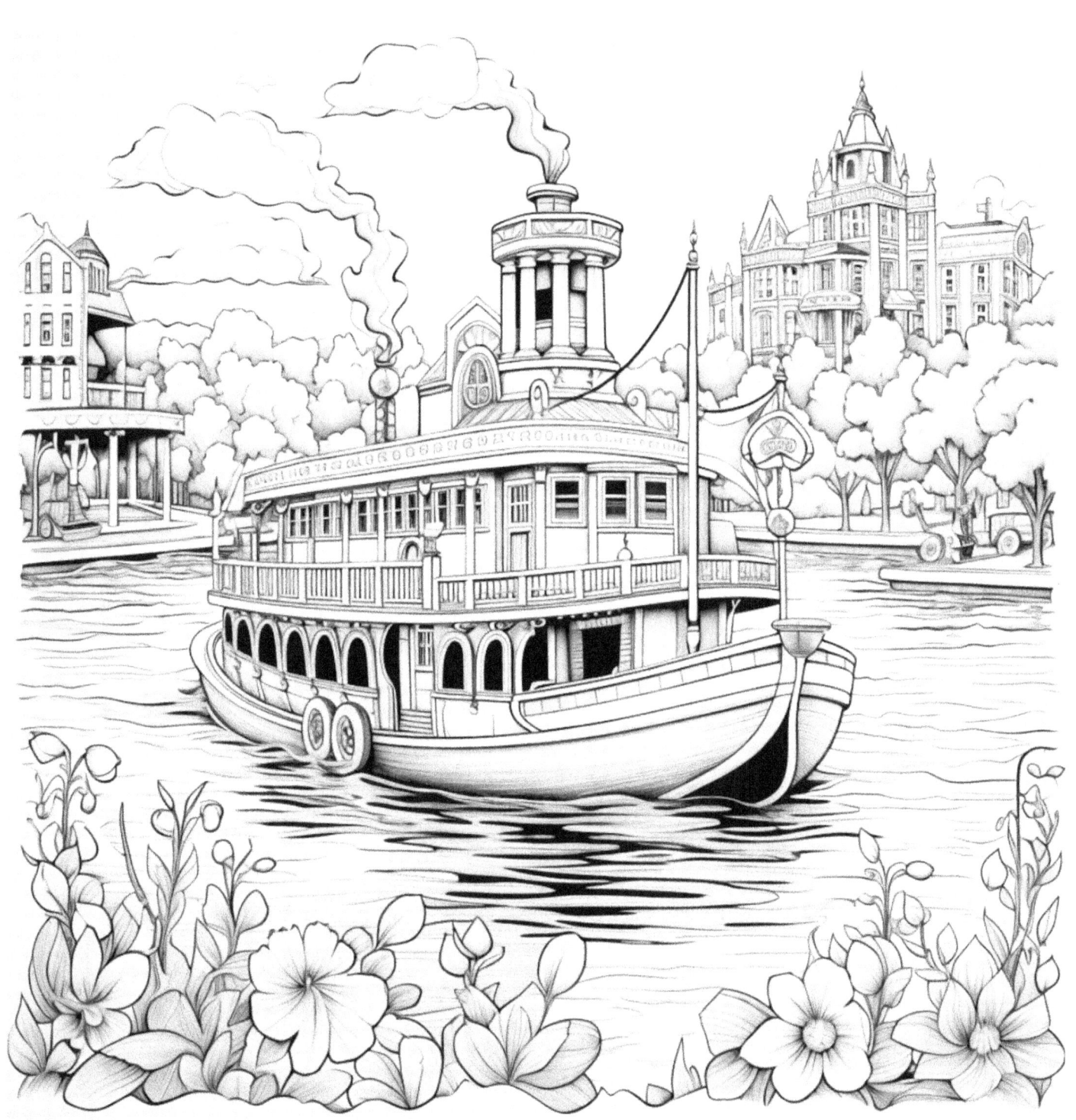

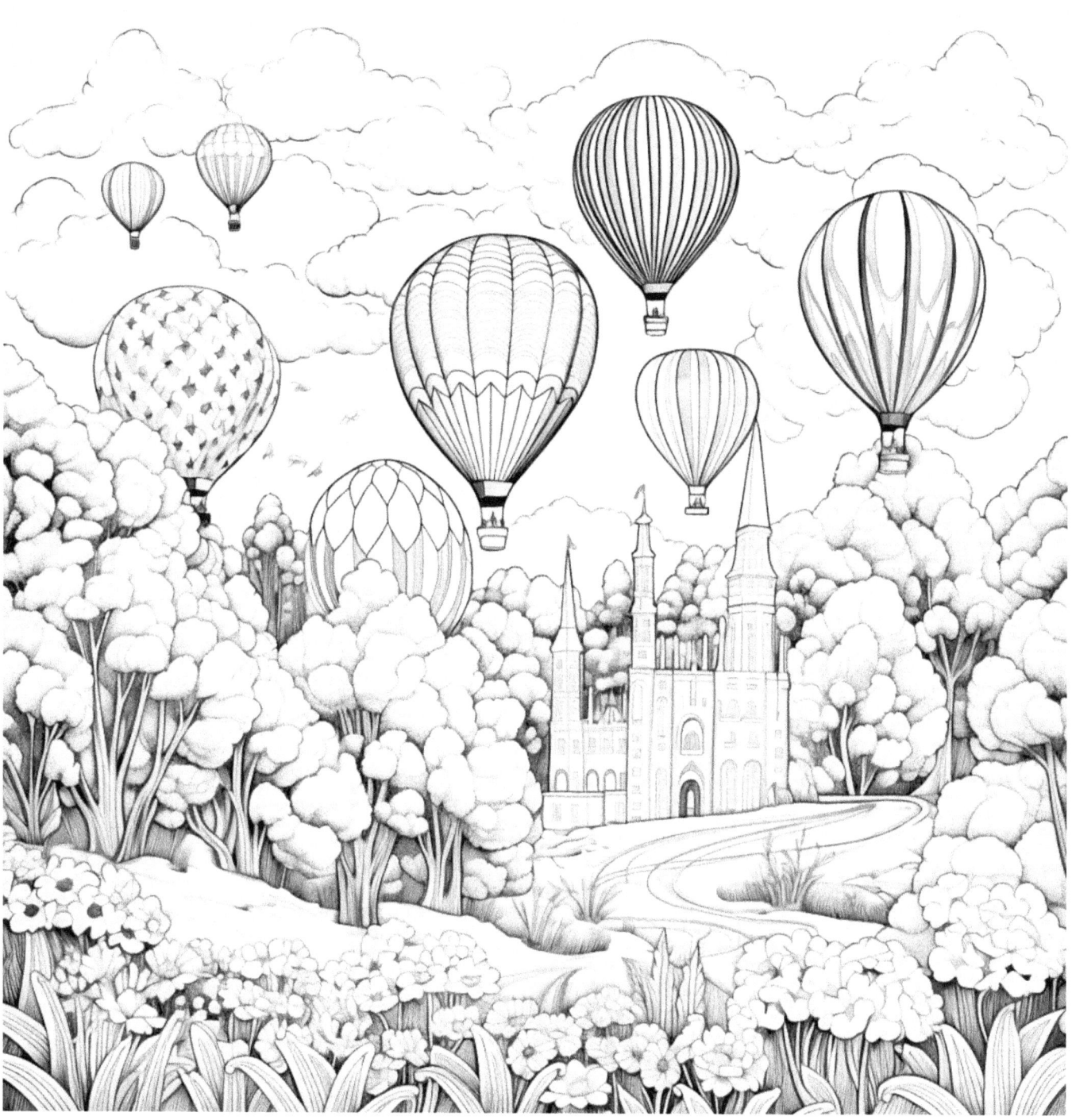

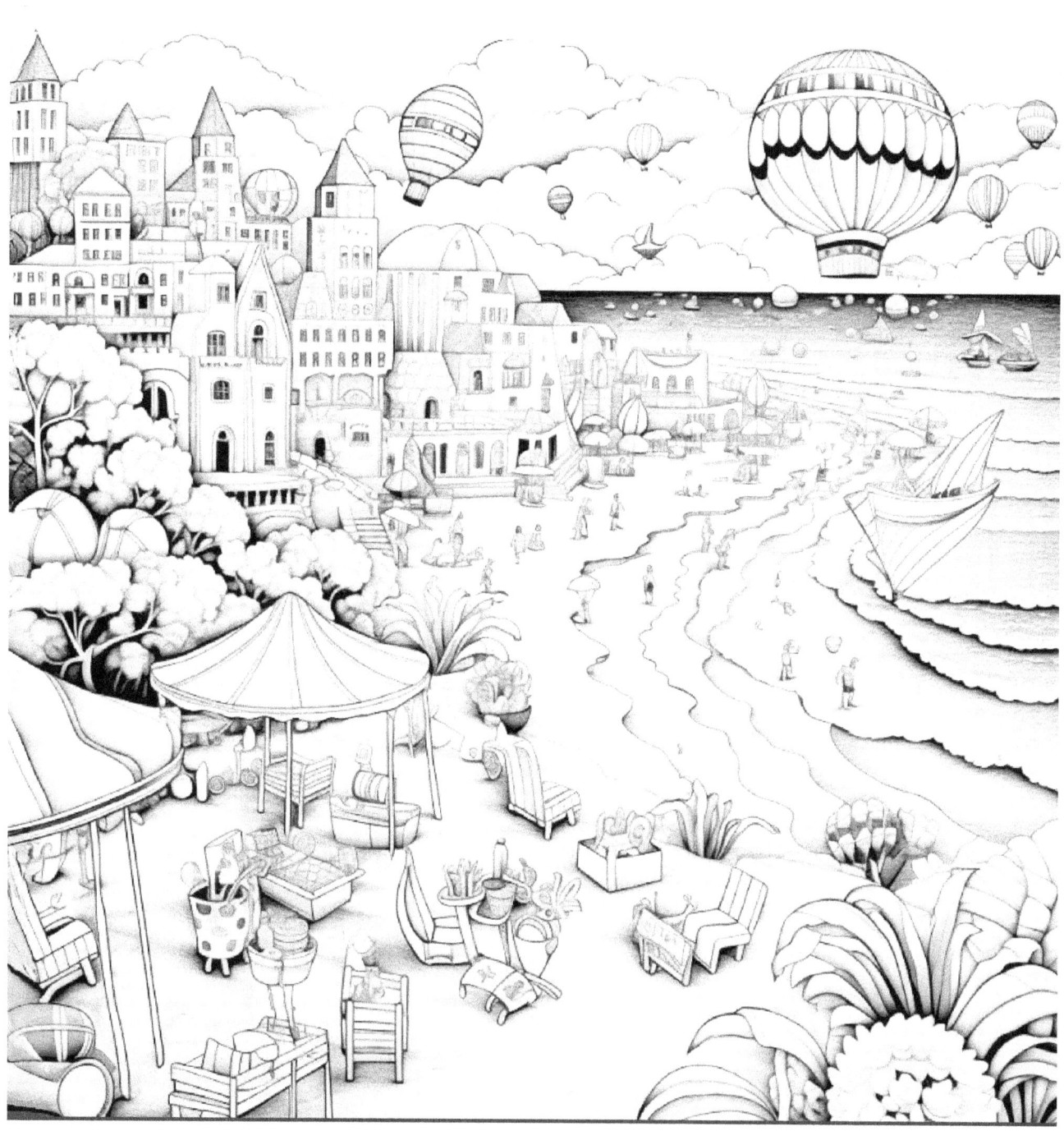

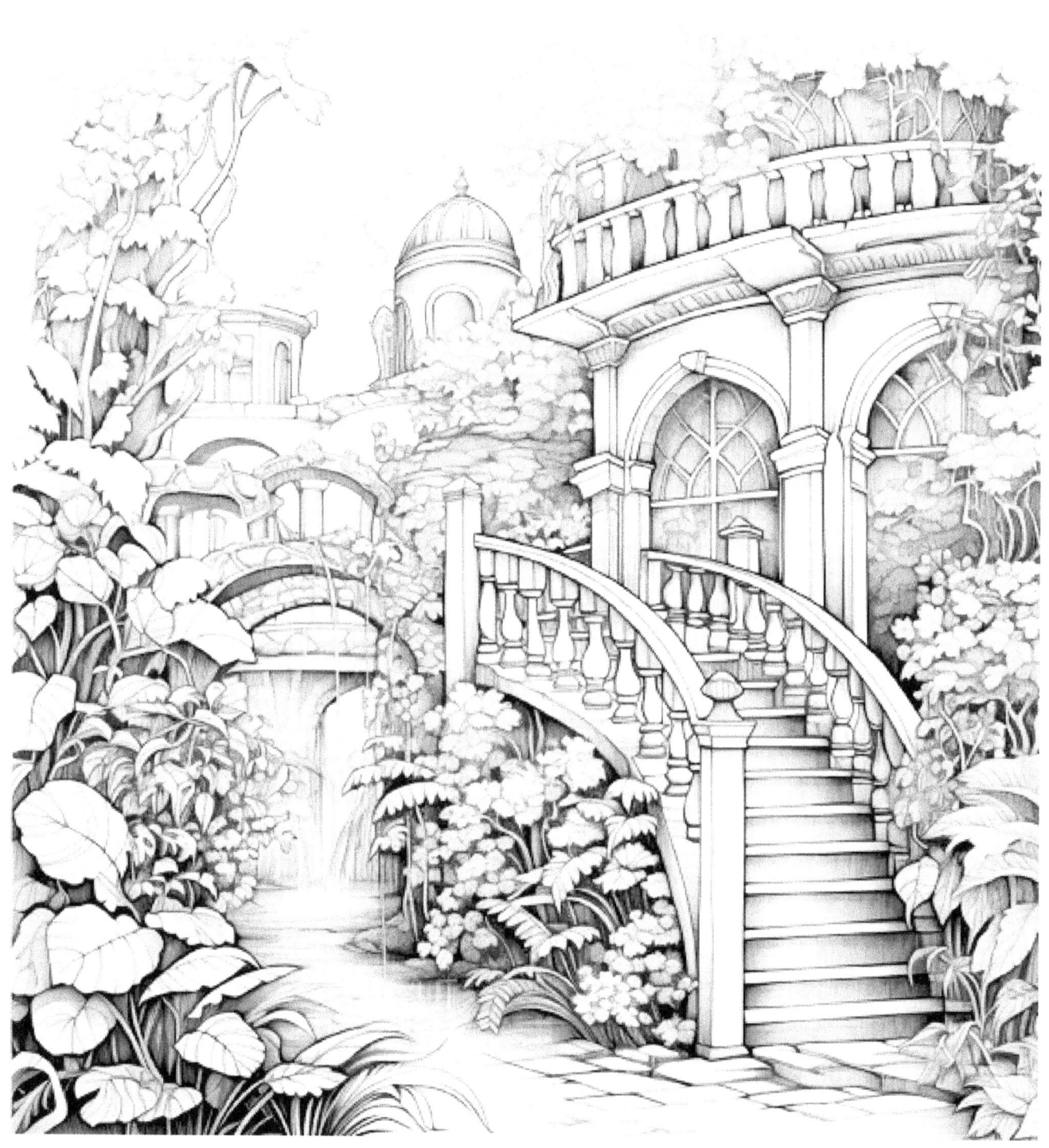

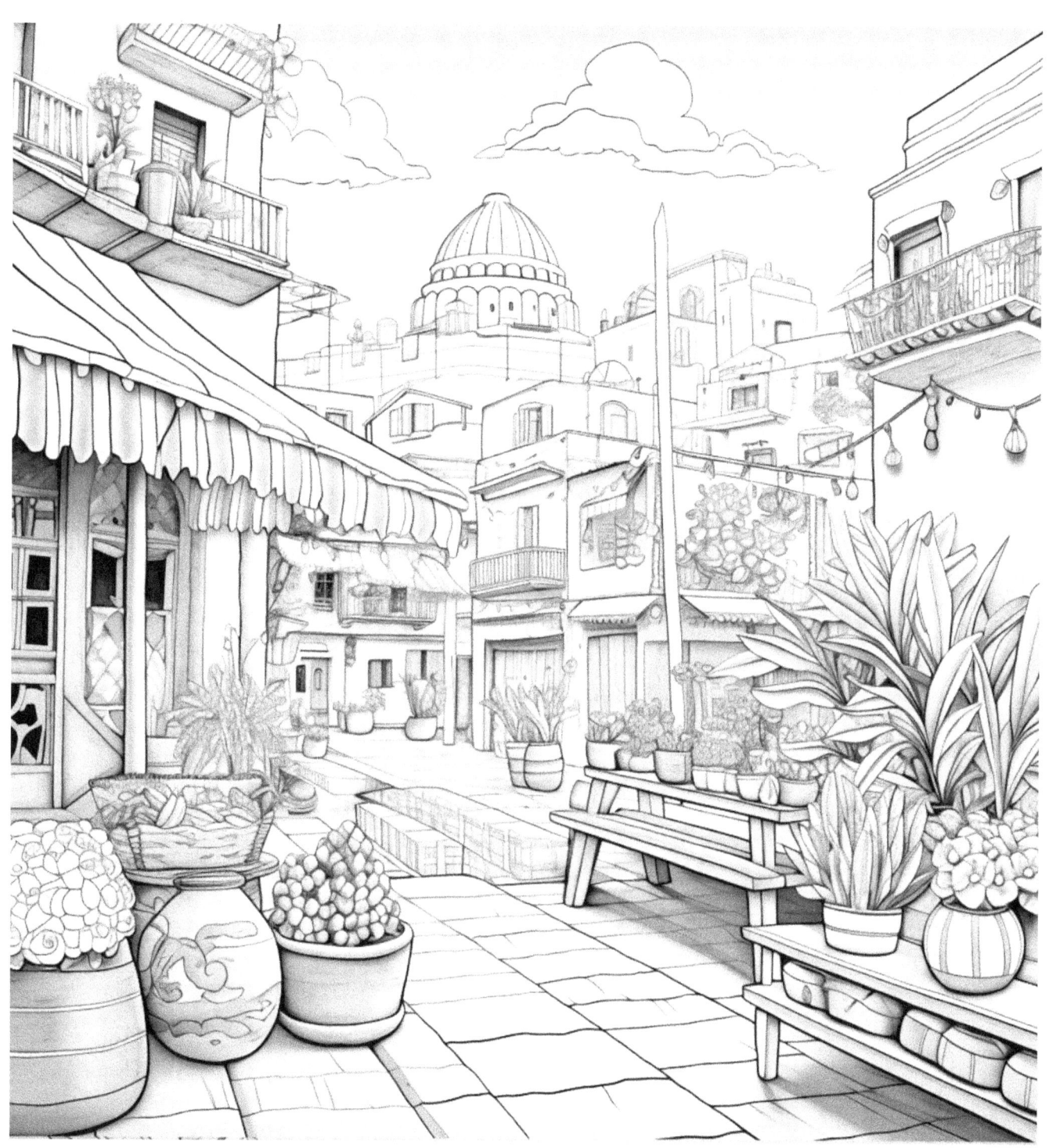

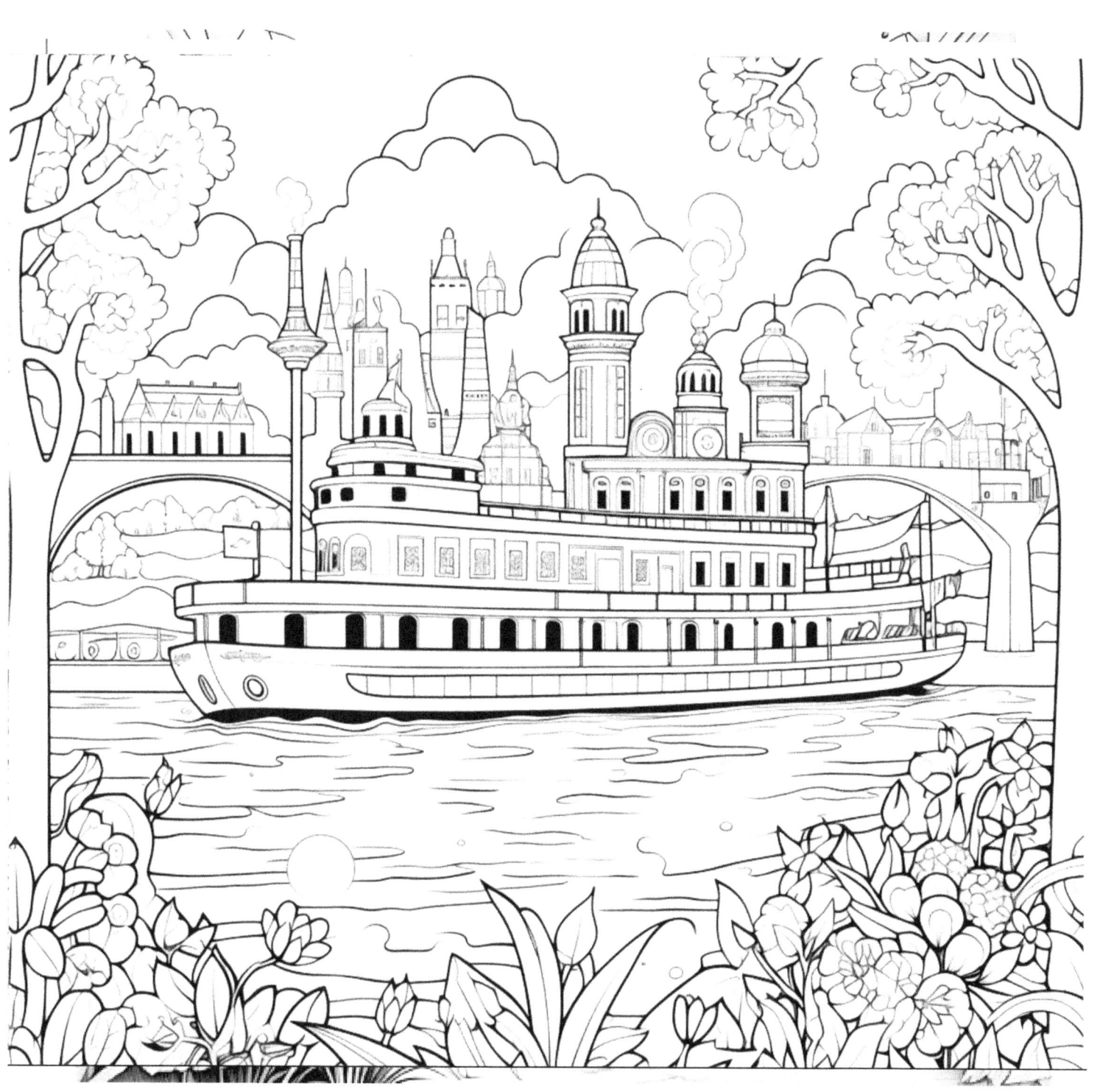

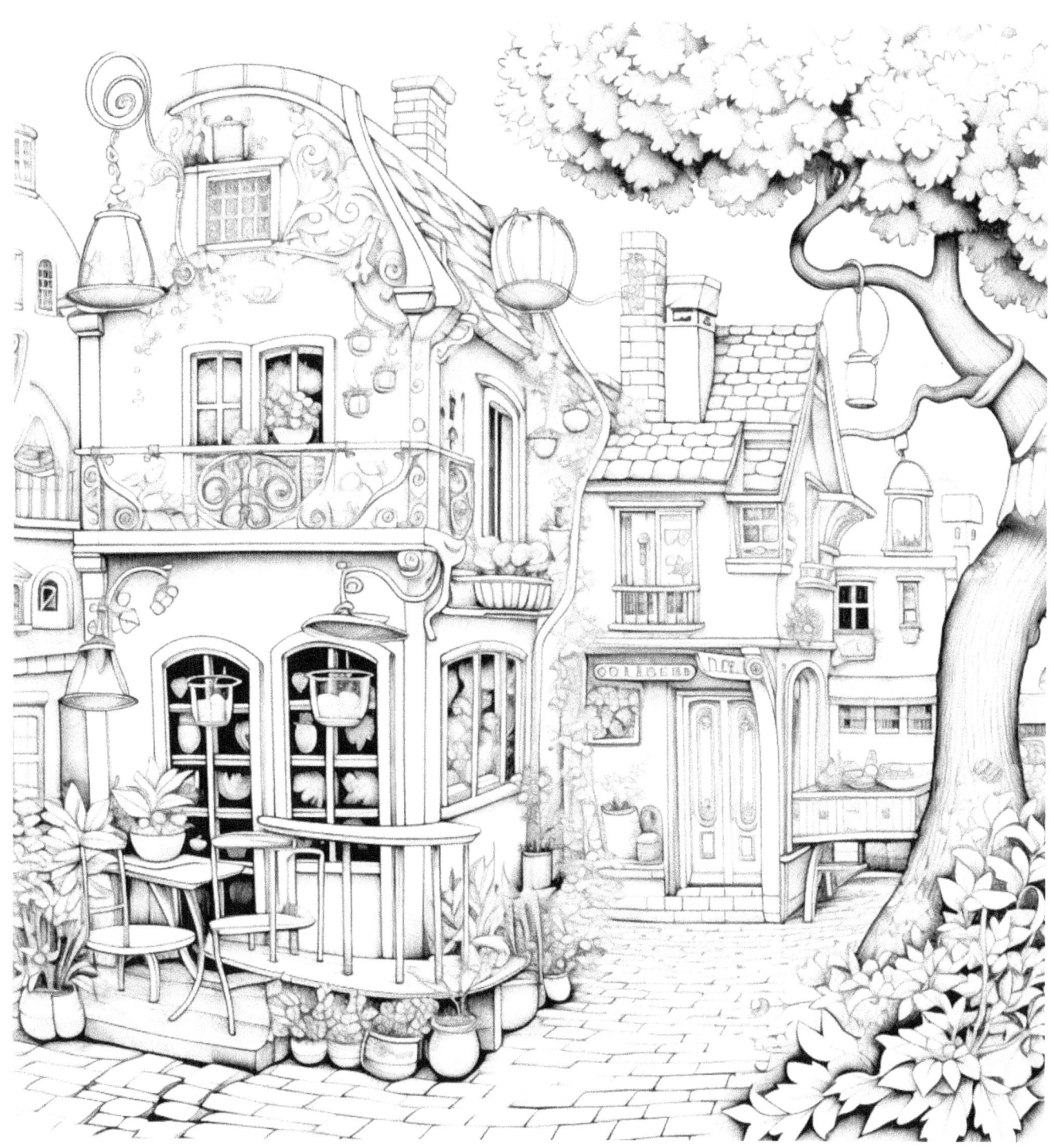

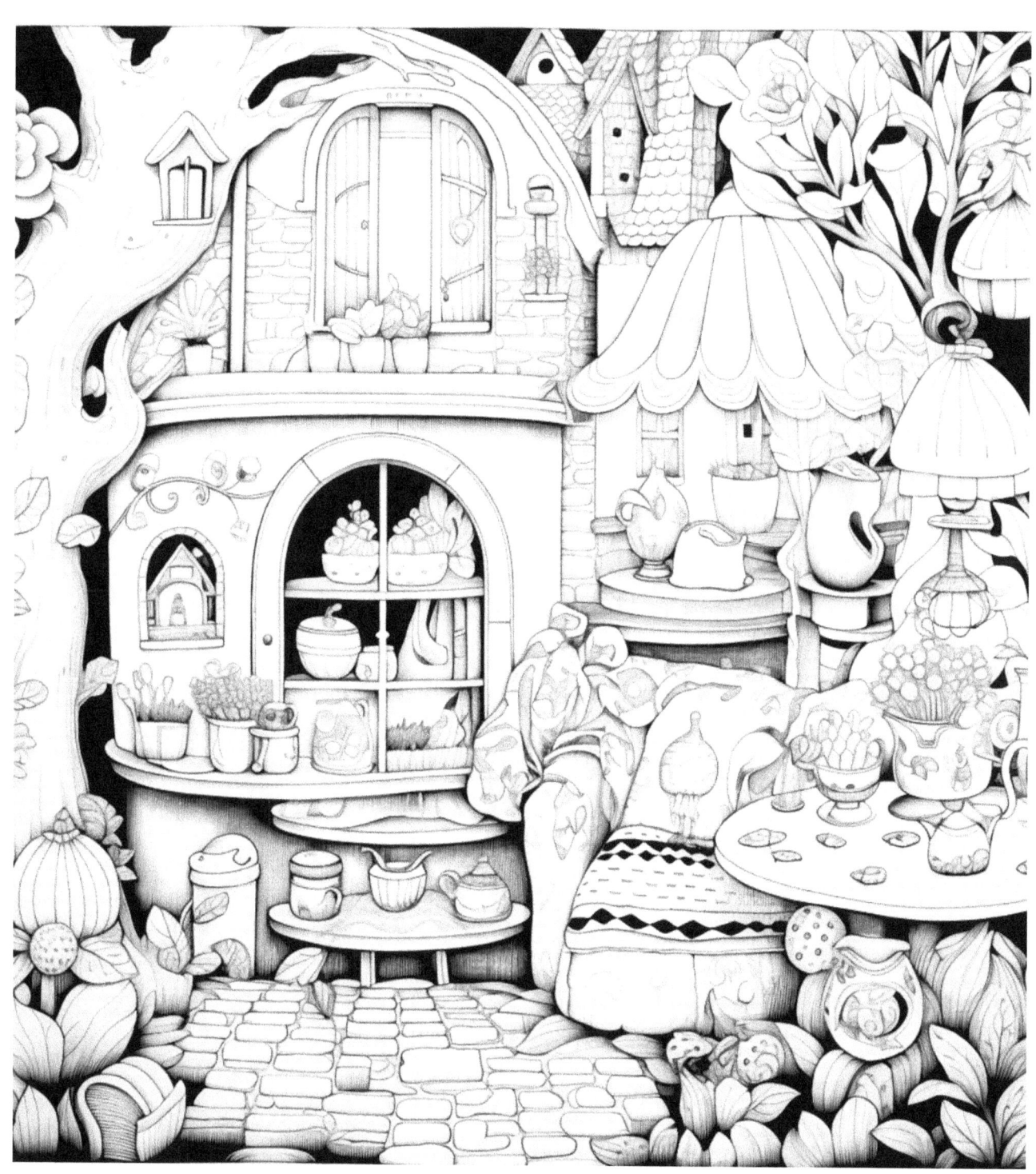

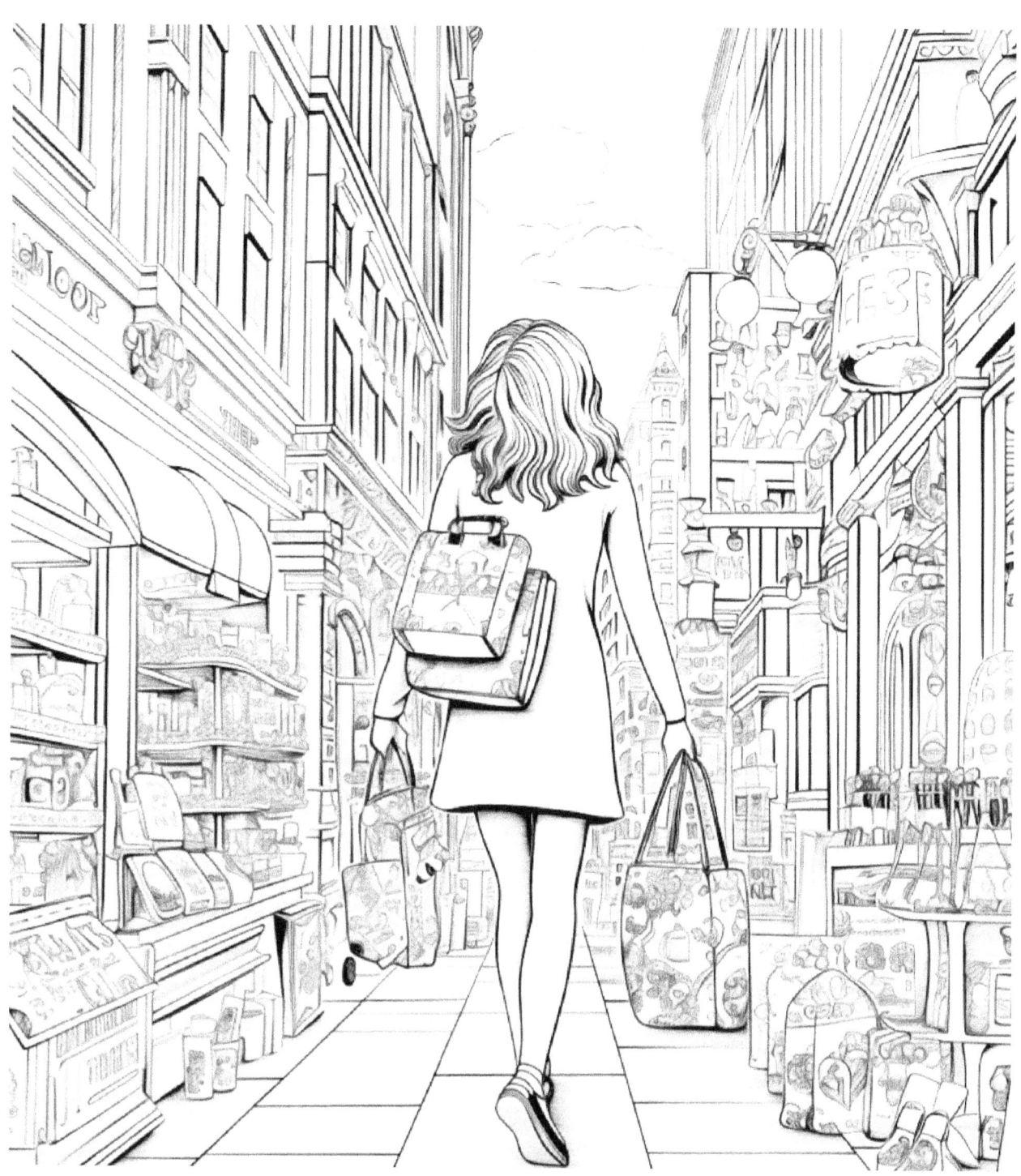

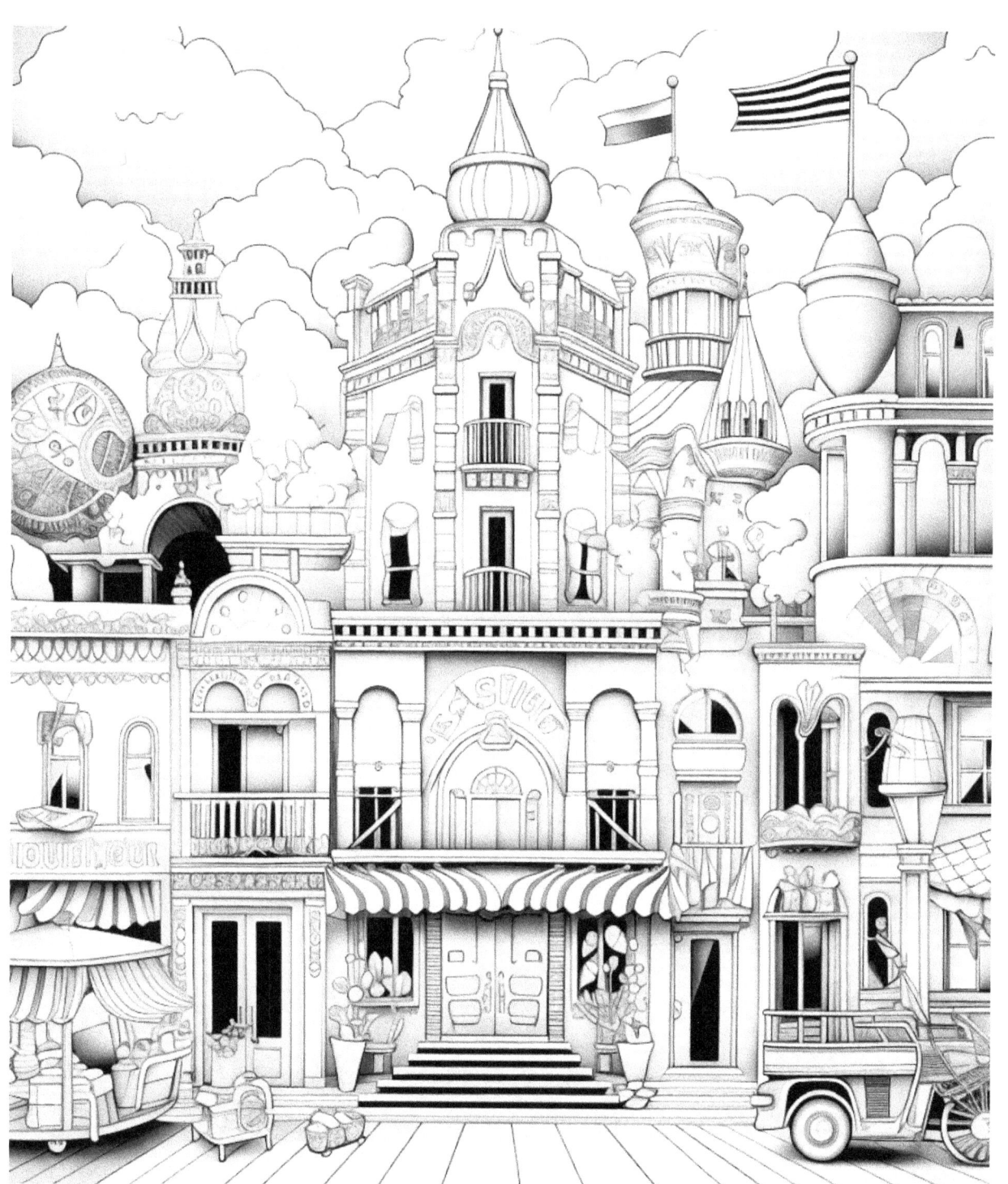

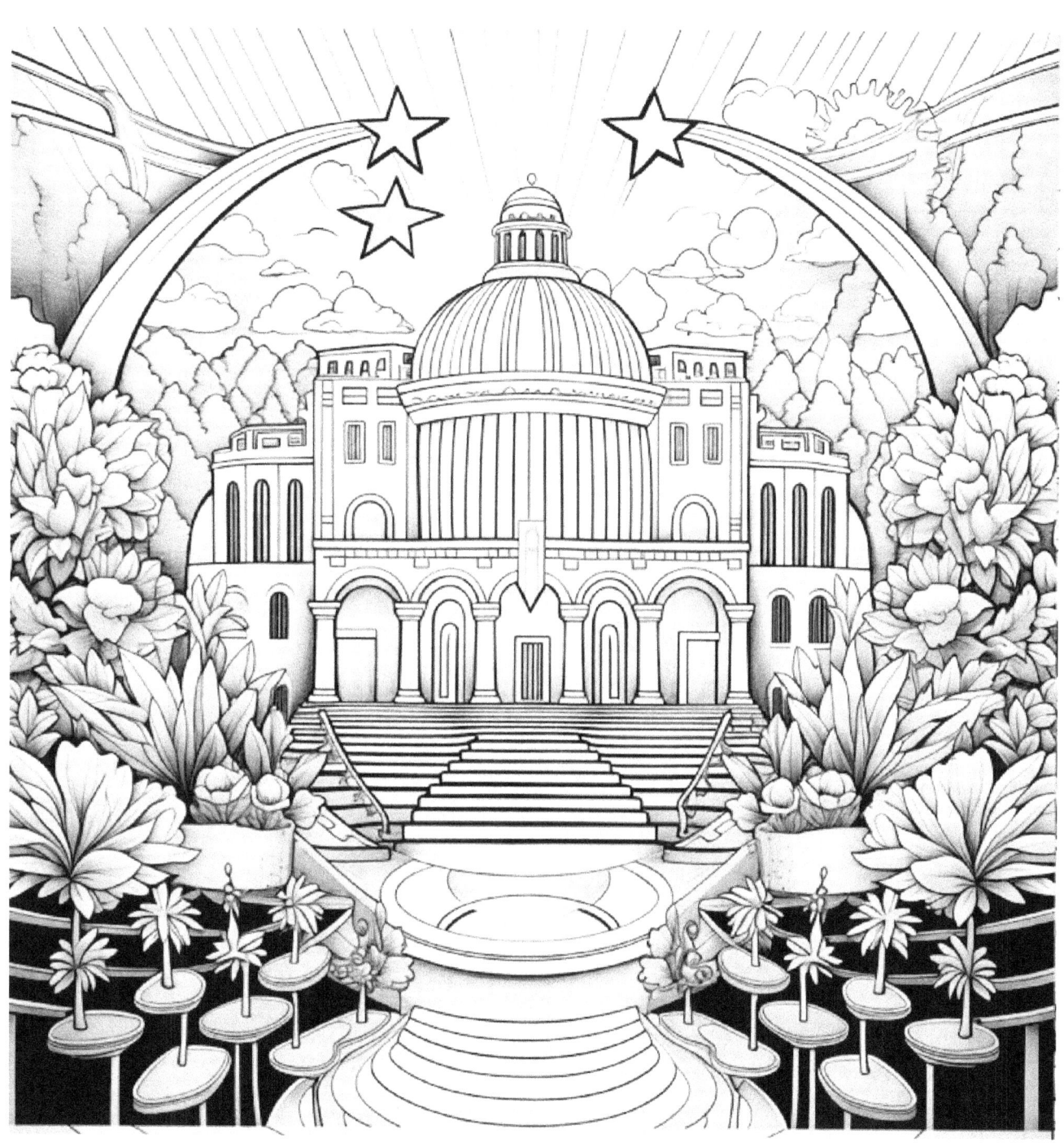

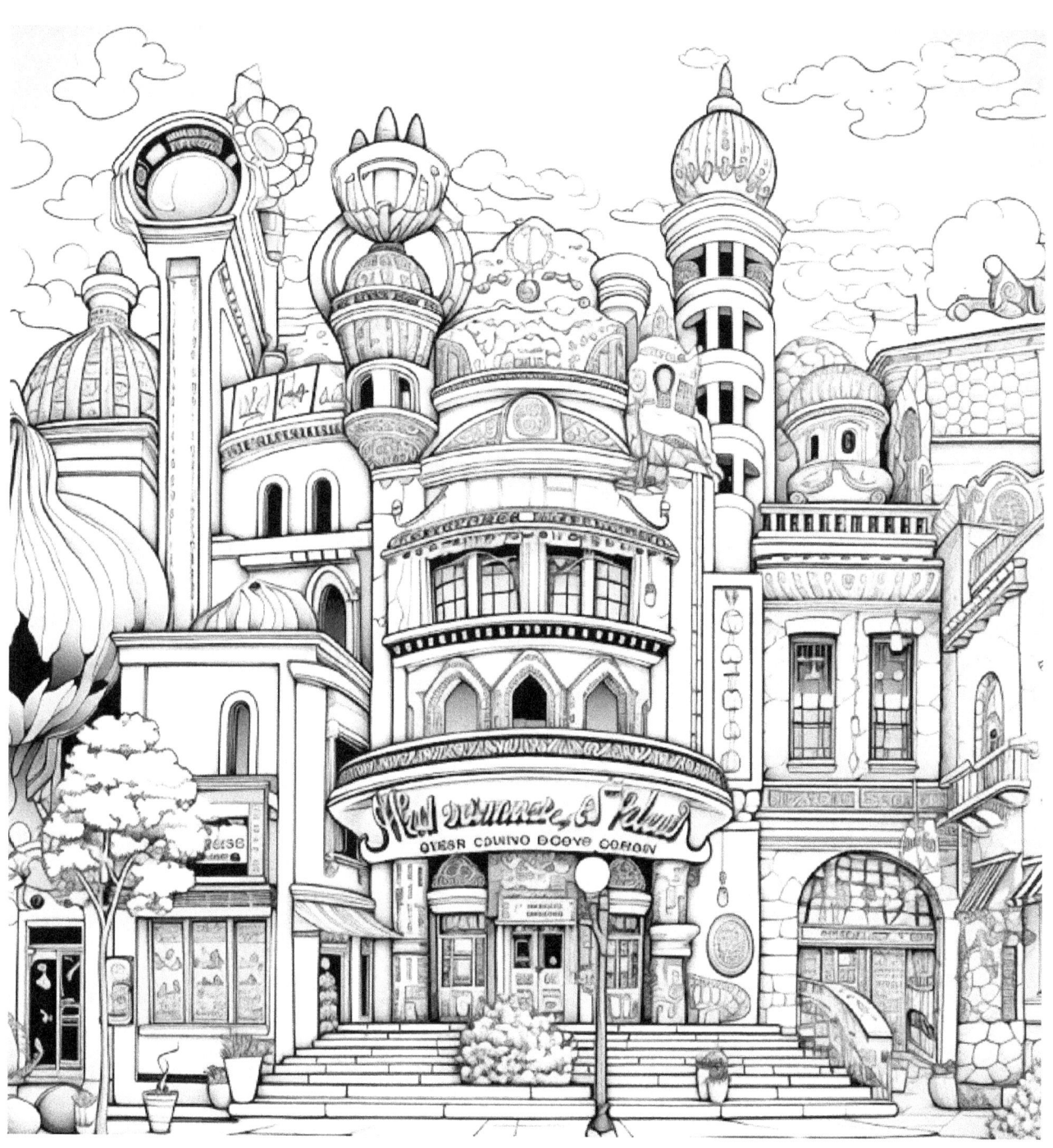

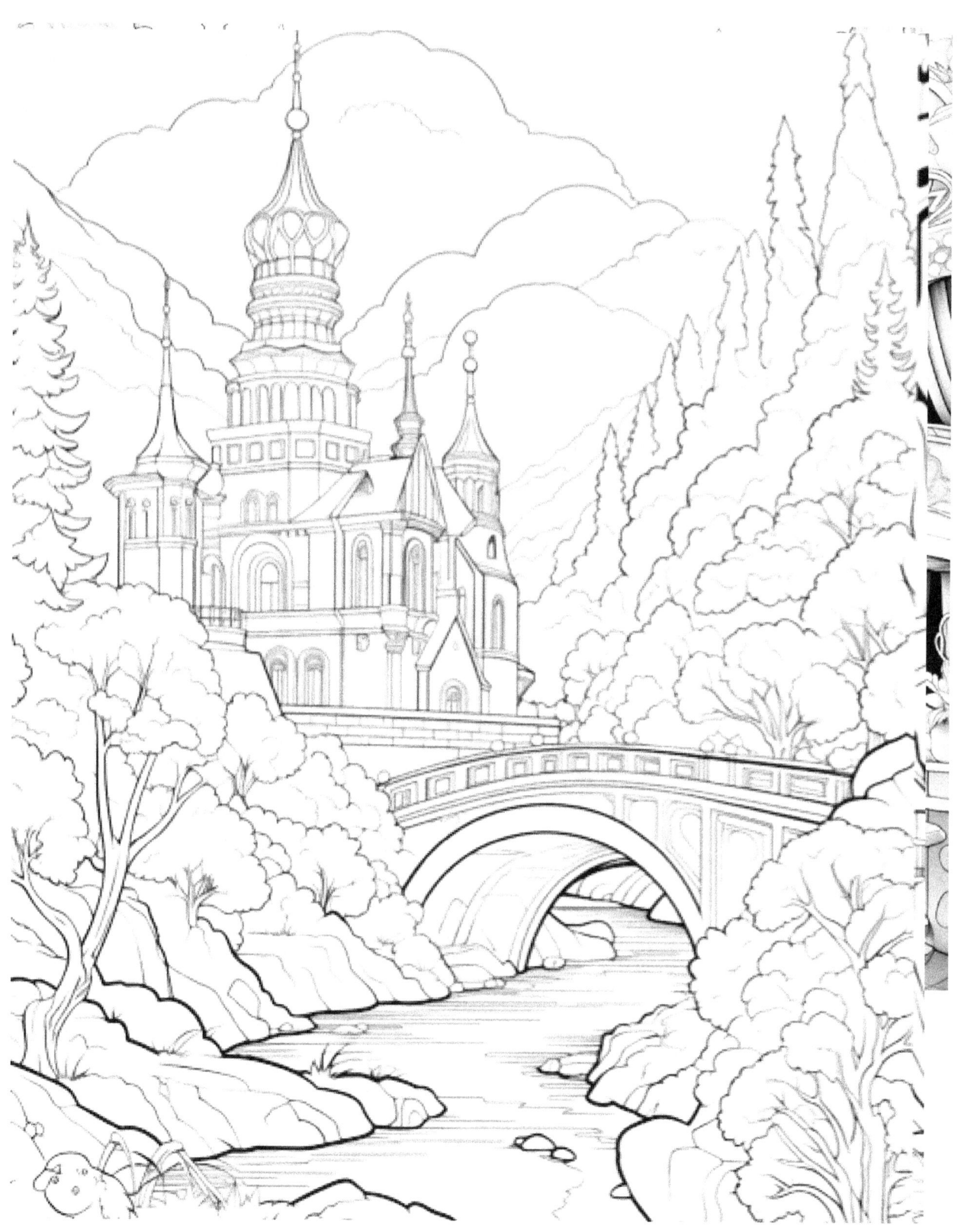

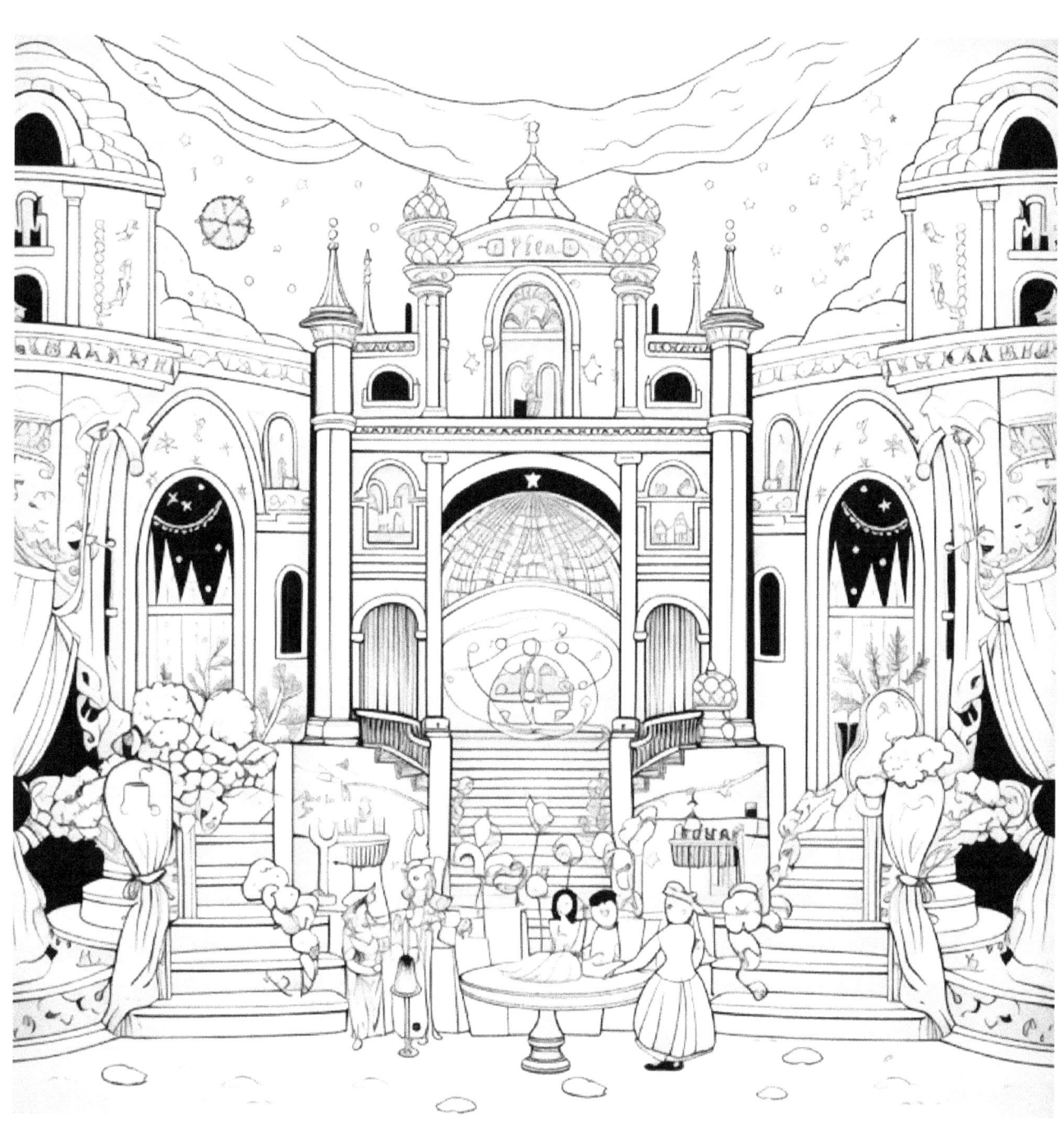

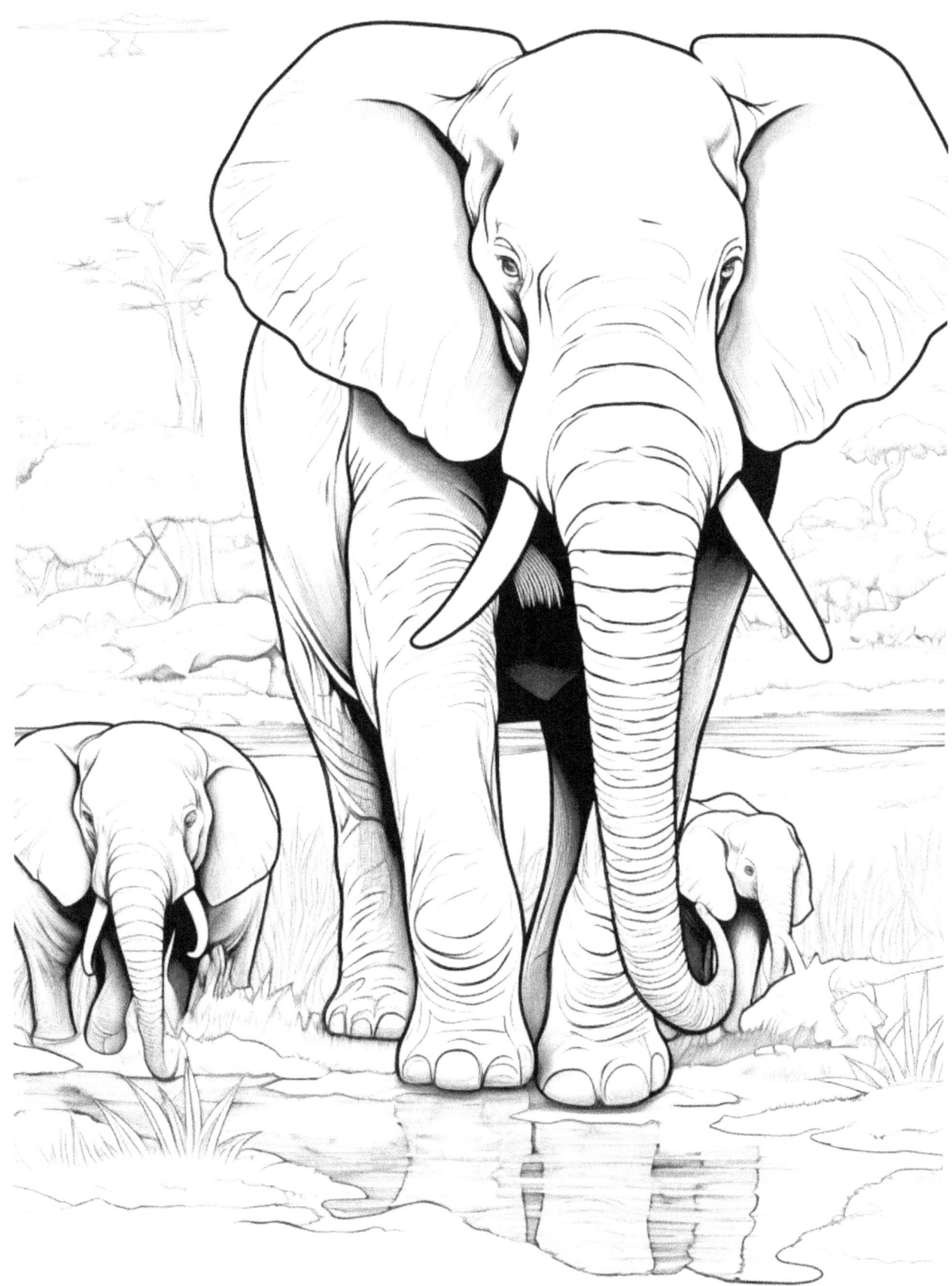

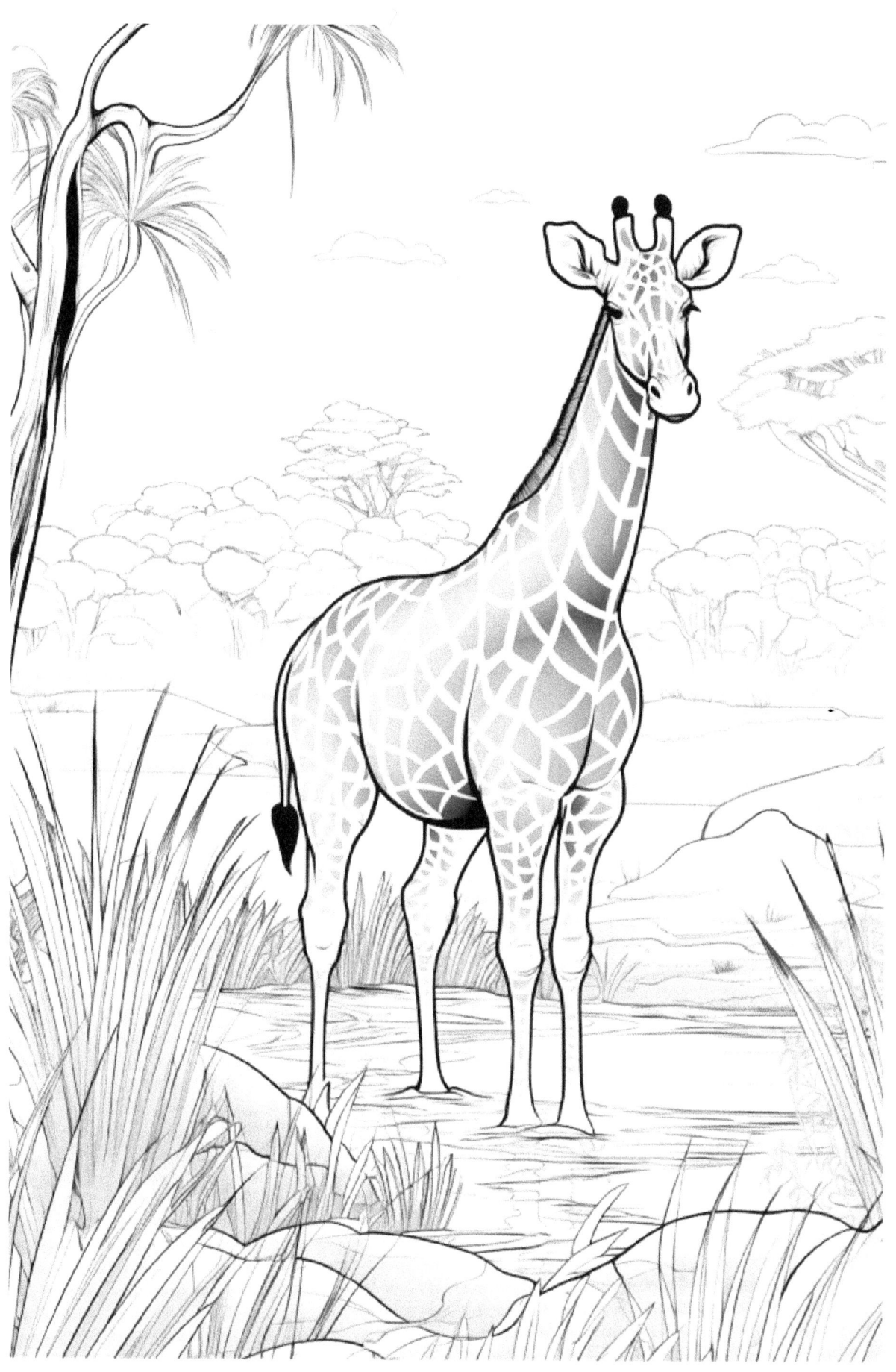

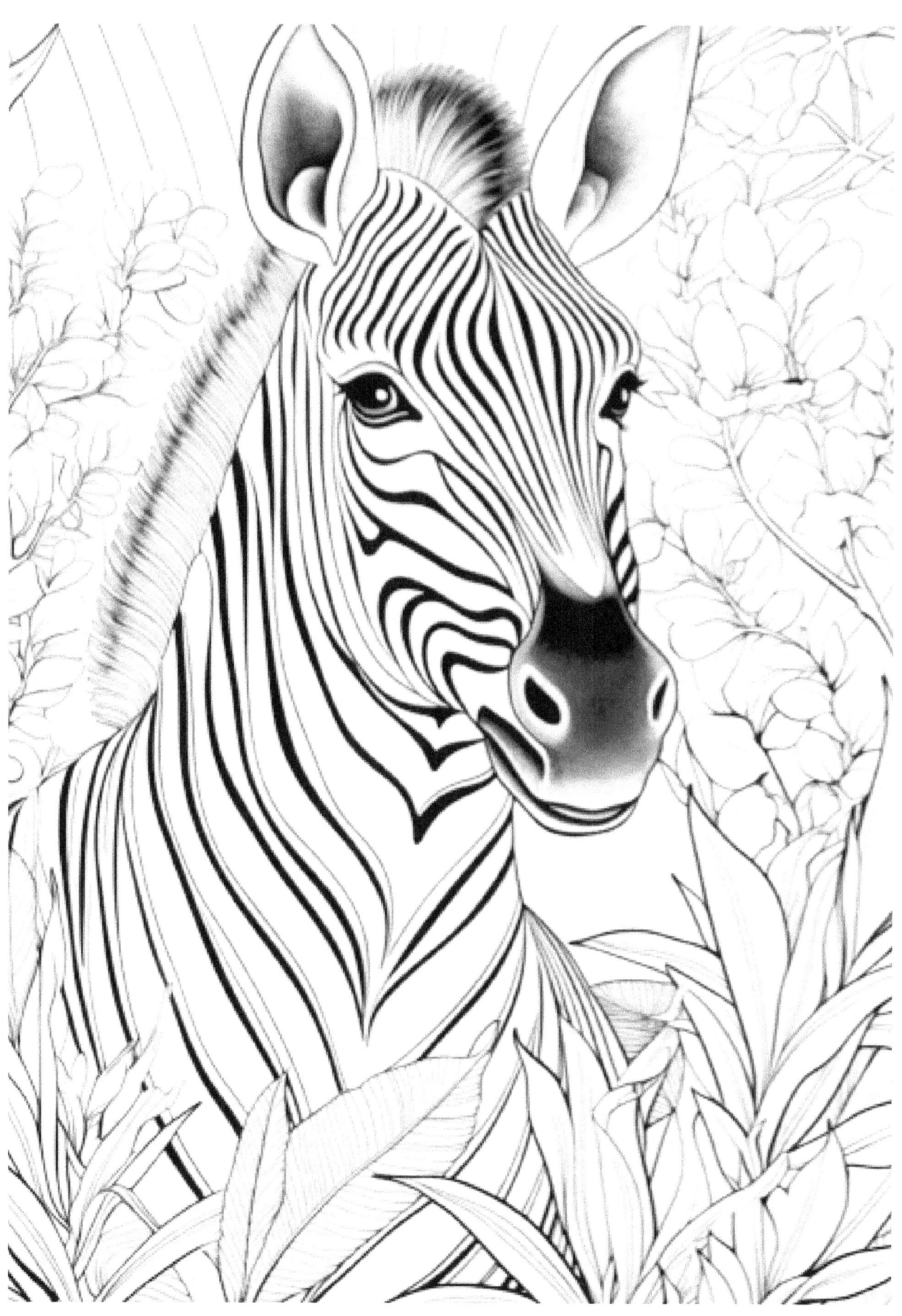

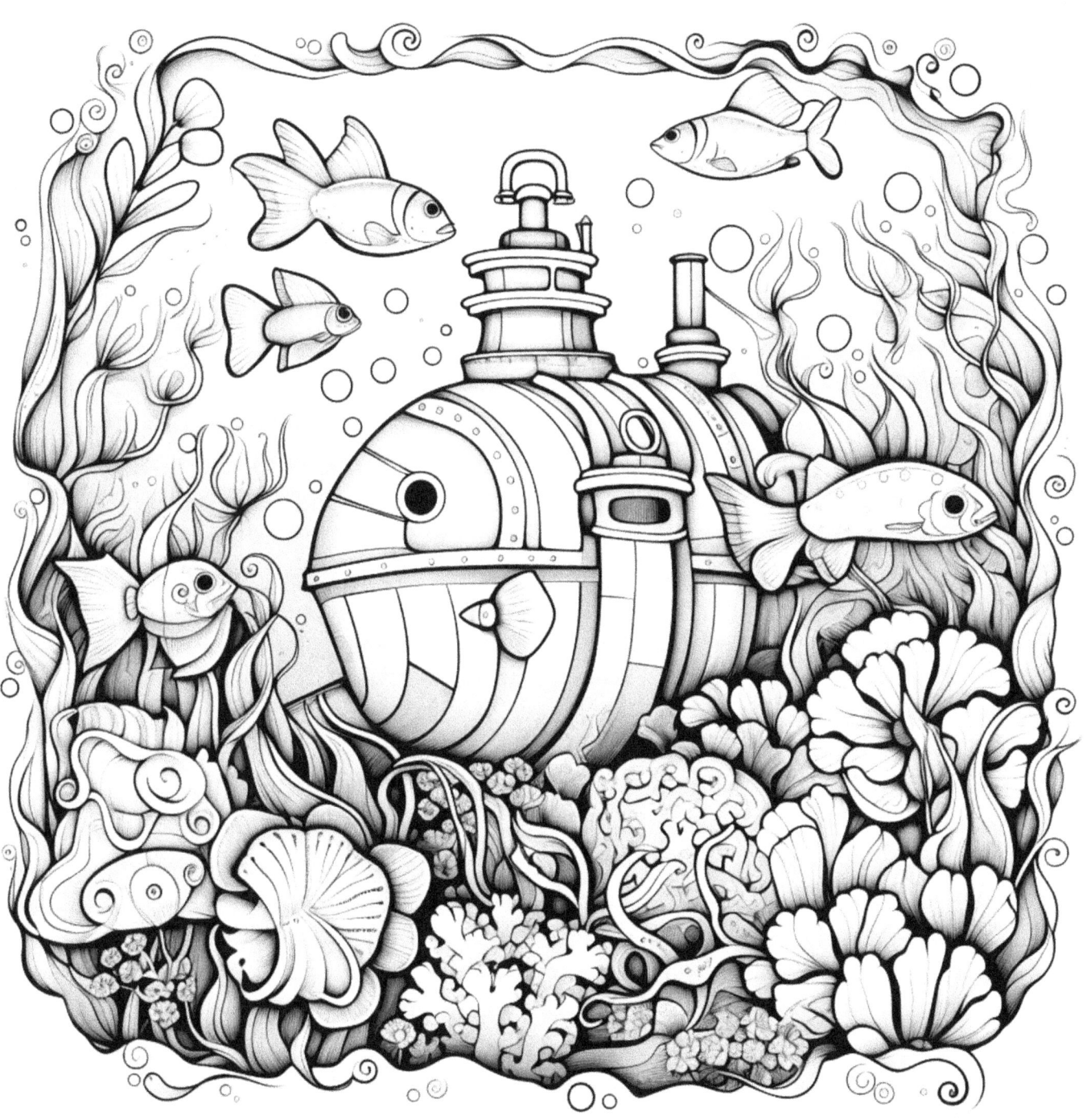

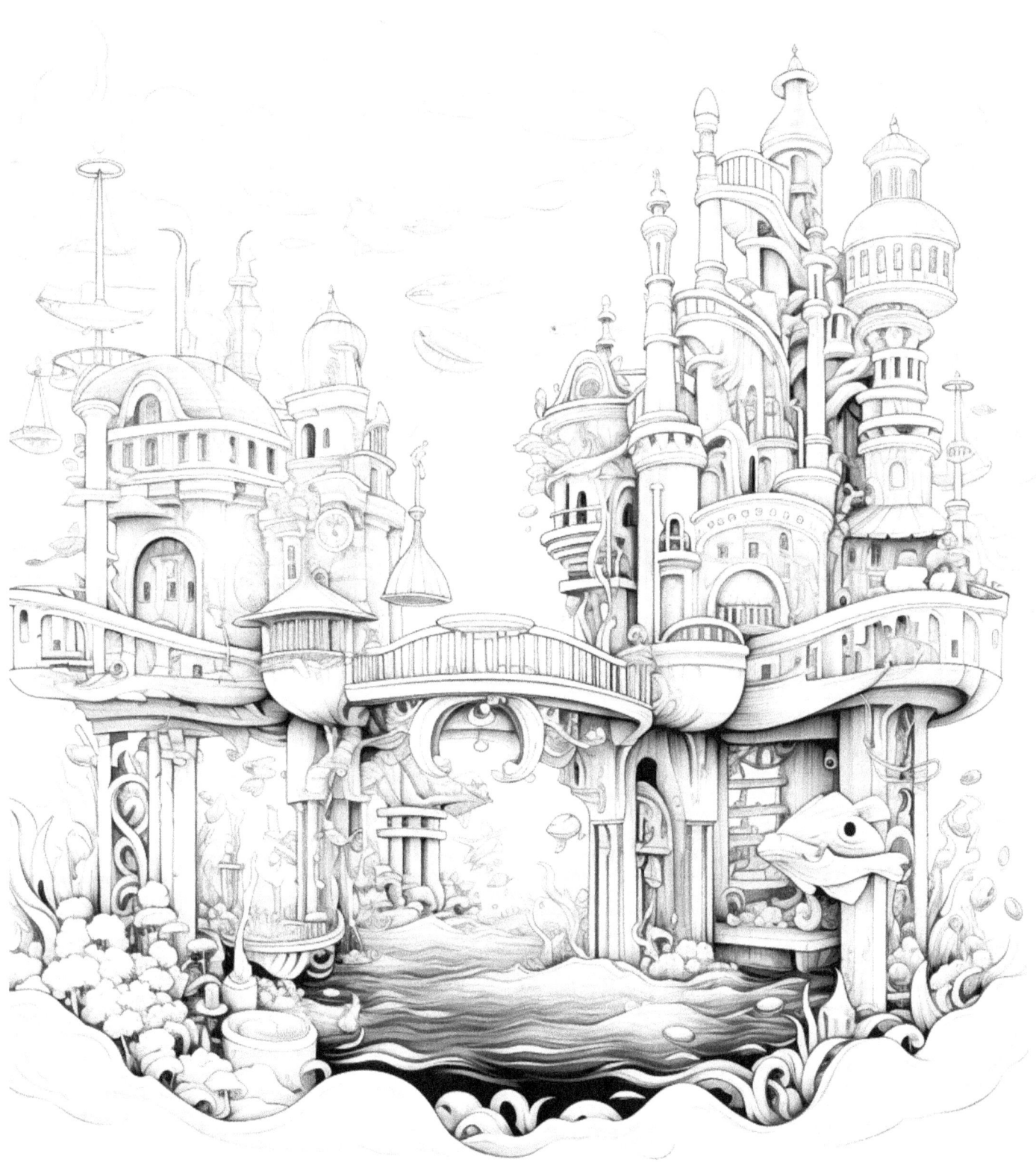

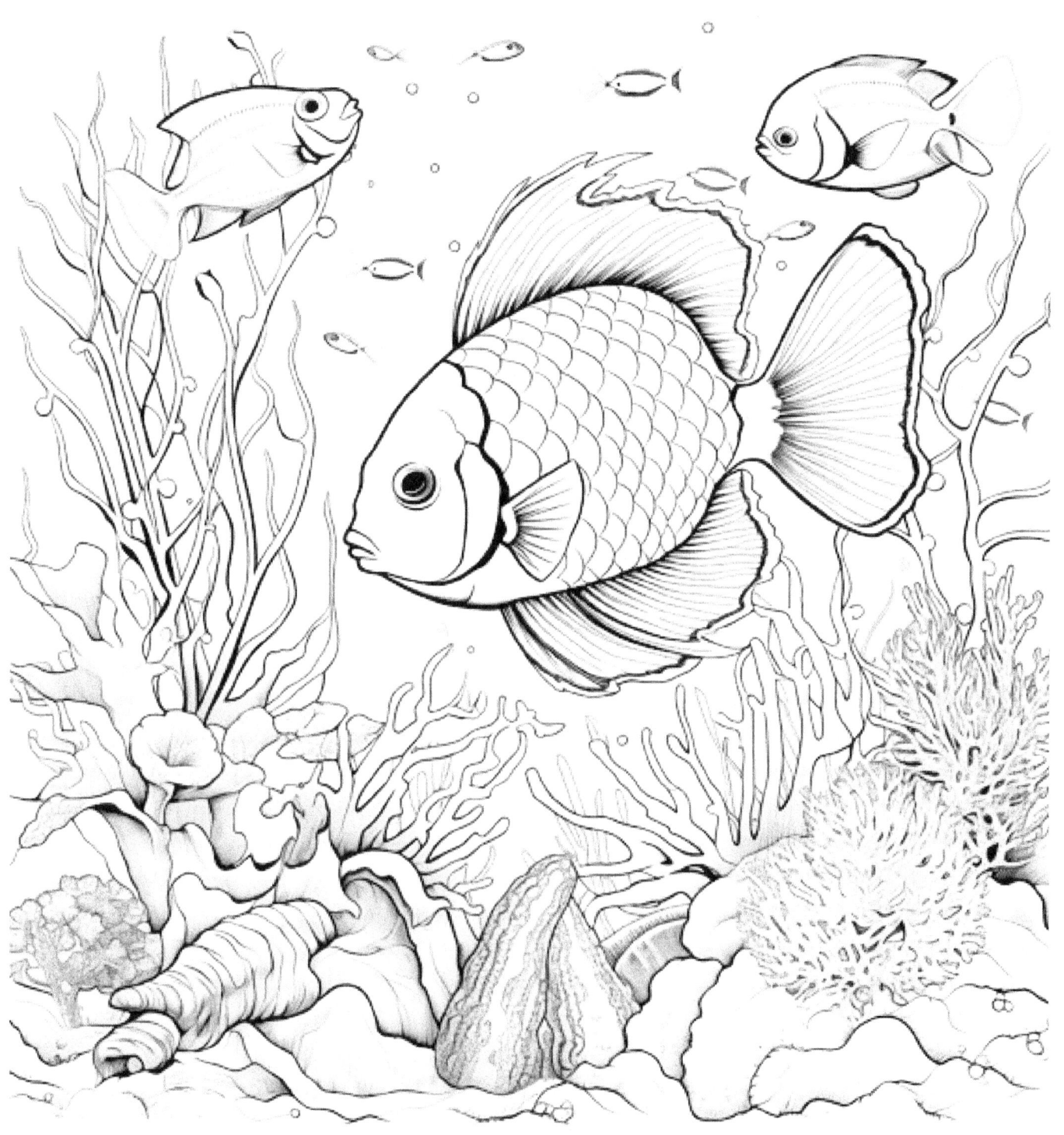

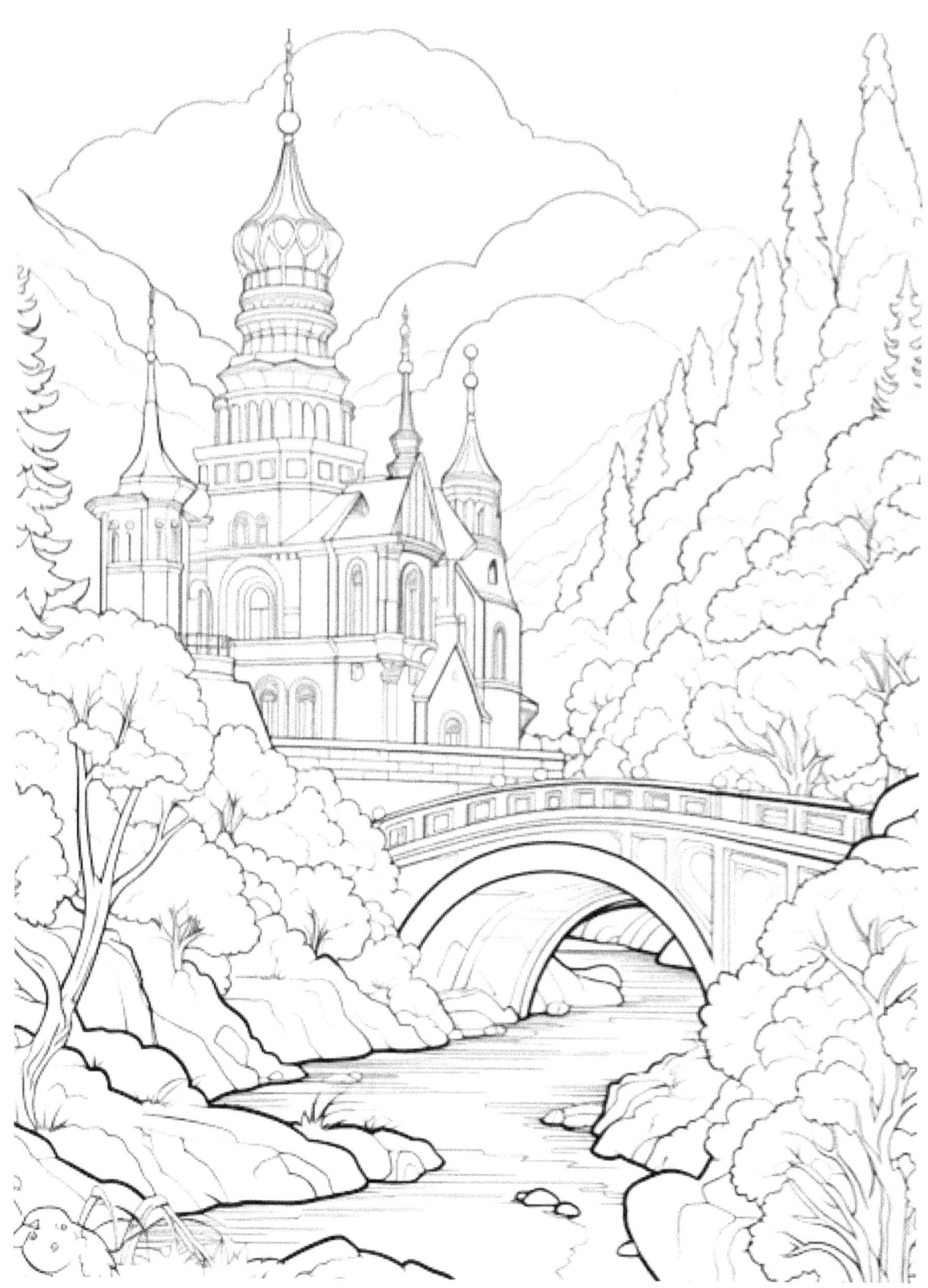

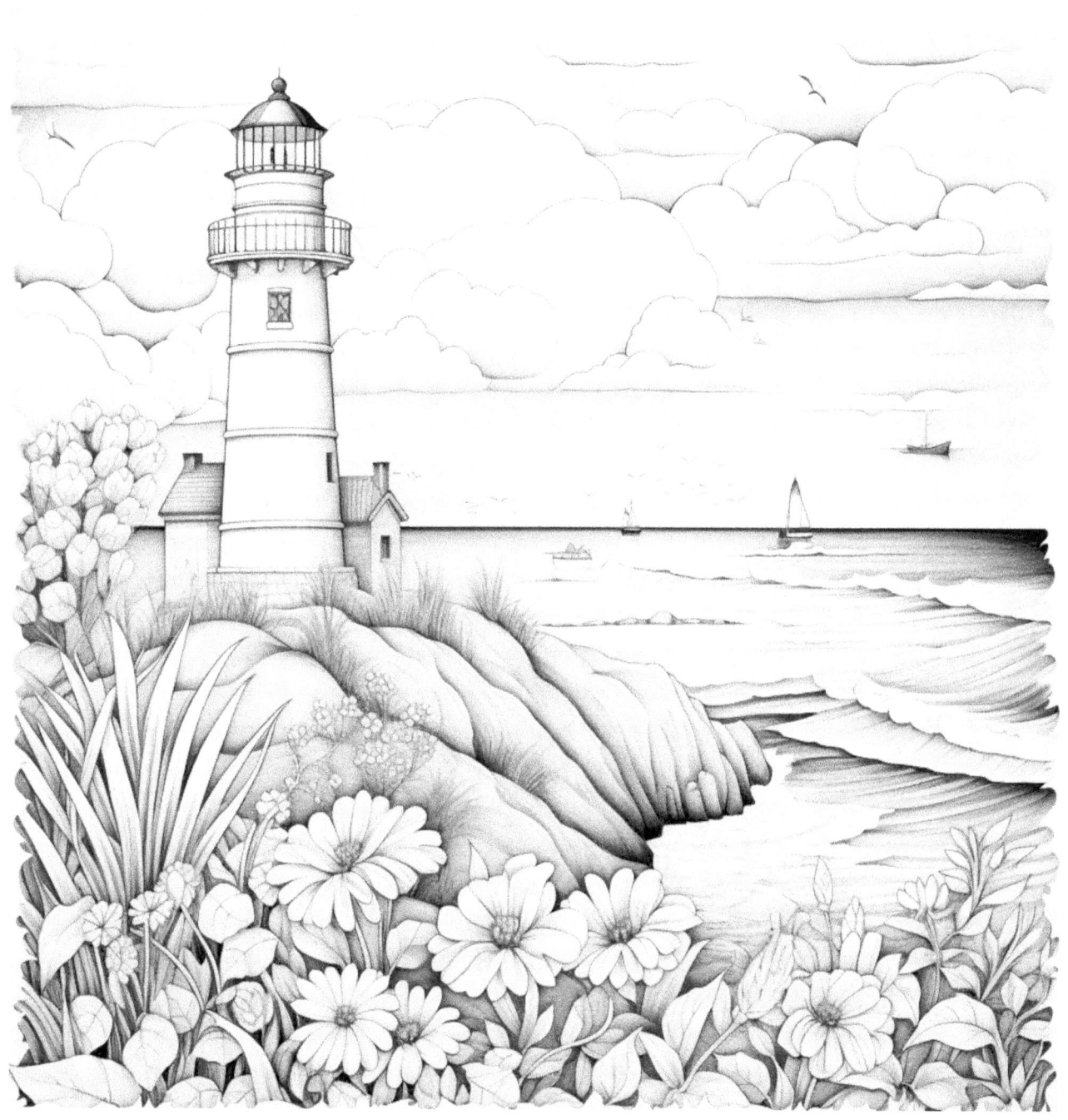

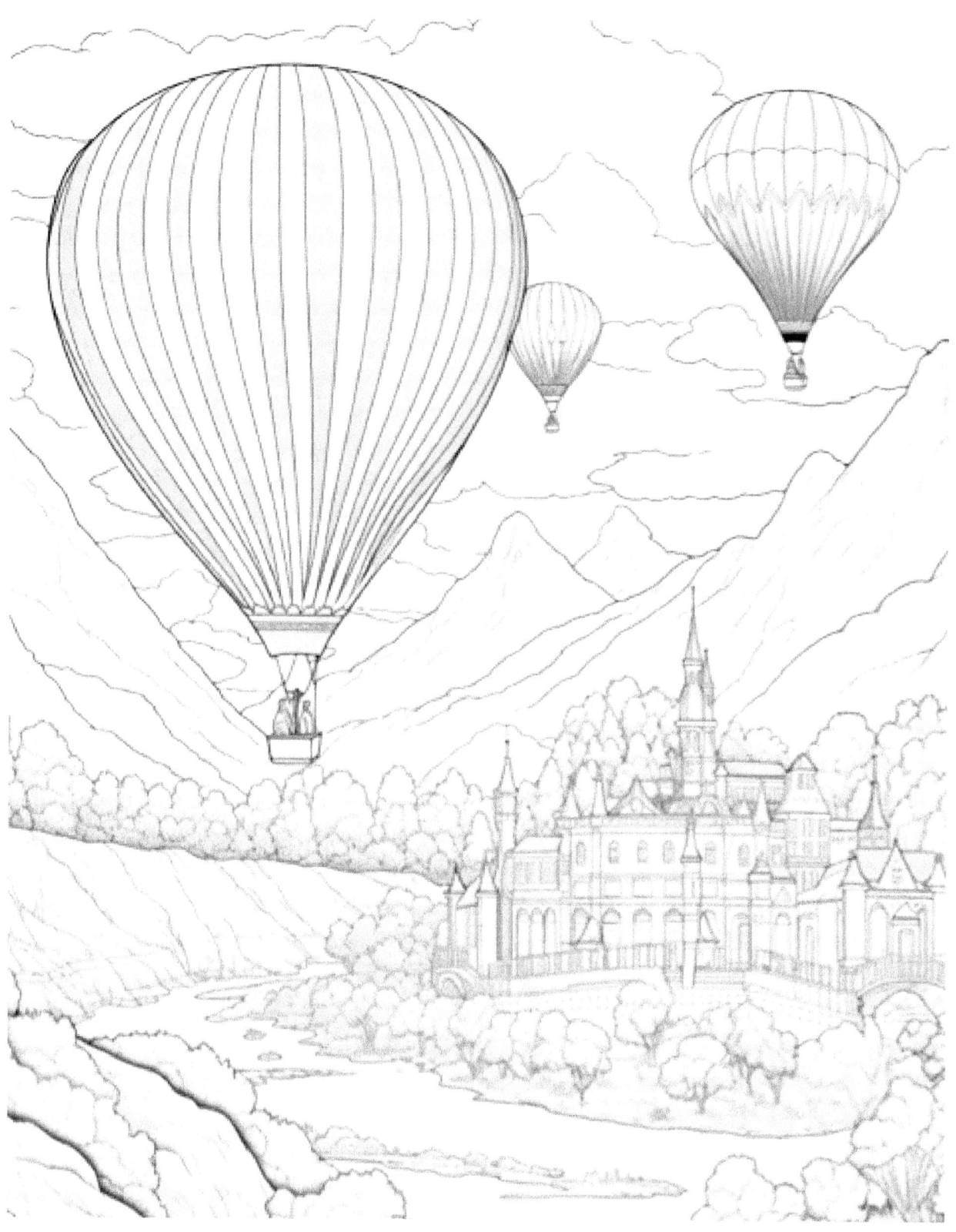

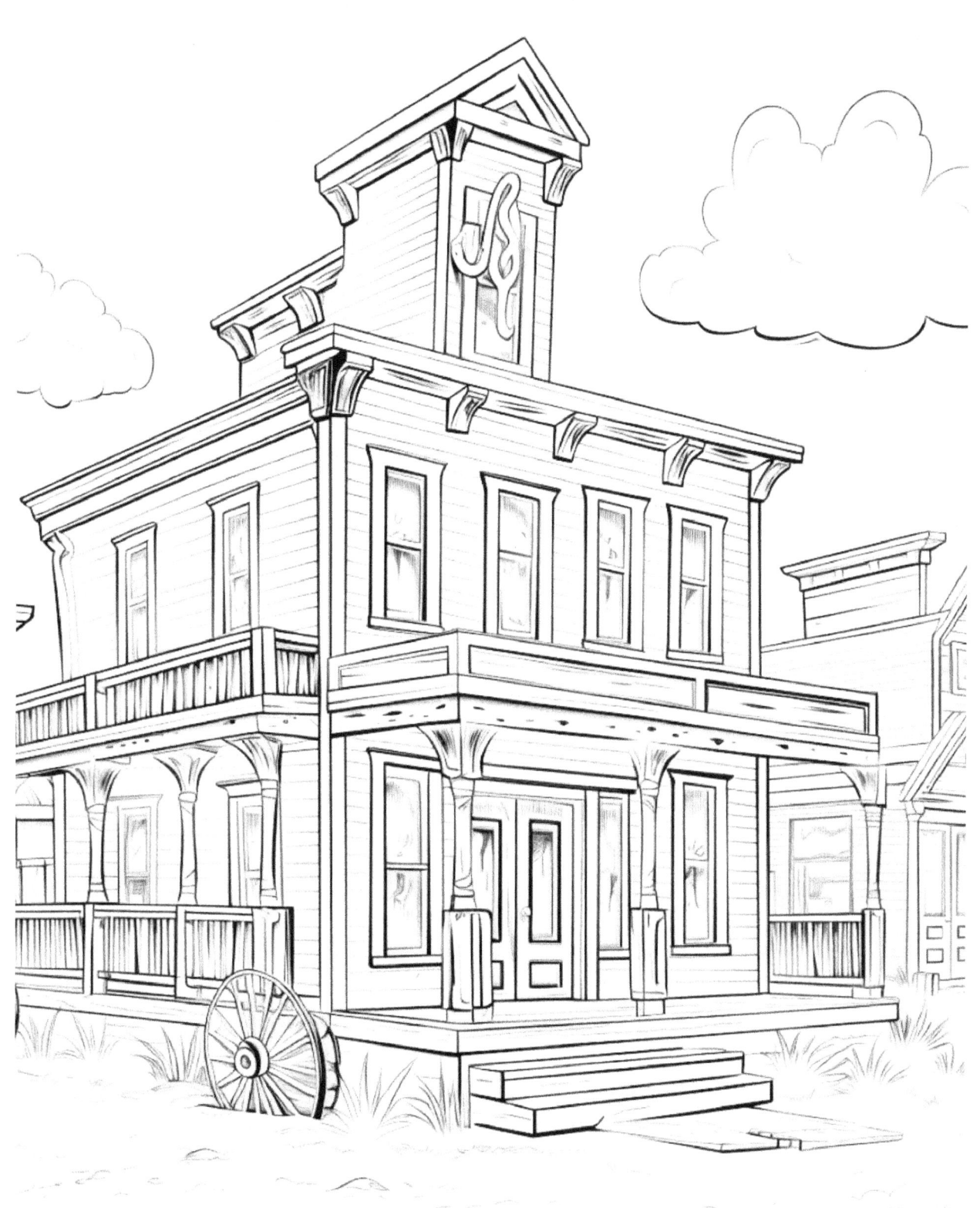

Your feedback is greatly appreciated!

It's through your feedback, support and reviews that we're able to create the best books possible and serve more people.

We would be extremely grateful if you could take just 60 seconds to kindly leave an honest review of the book on Amazon. Please share your feedback and thoughts for others to see.

To do so, simply find the book on Amazon's website (or wherever you purchased the book from) and locate the section to leave a review. Select a star rating and write a couple of sentences.

That's it! Thank you so much for your support.

Review this product

Share your thoughts with other customers

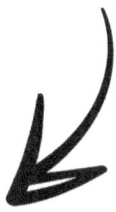

Write a customer review

www.ingramcontent.com/pod-product-compliance
Lightning Source LLC
Chambersburg PA
CBHW081203290526
45796CB00010B/326